TIMELESS
Trivia

TIMELESS

TIMELESS *Trivia*

Volume Six

JUNIOR EDITION

1000 Questions, Teasers and Stumpers
for the Young and Young-At-Heart

by
**JOCI BARNES, JACKSON BOUSTEAD,
PARKER CARMAN, JOHNATHAN EVANS,
MASON FUNES, SAWYER FUNES,
LUCY GRIFFITH, BOB HAMMITT**

Edited by
CHRIS BANGS AND LINCOLN BANGS

Timeless Trivia: Volume Six

FROM THE AUTHOR

Thank you for purchasing "Timeless Trivia Volume Six: Junior Edition!" We hope that the young and young-at-heart enjoy this book!

The "Timeless Trivia" book series began during the early stages of the Covid 19 pandemic, sort of by accident. I (Bob) am a high school social studies teacher. Within a few days of the initial lockdown, students and former students started reaching out to me about the immense boredom they were facing. They suggested that I host a daily trivia contest on Instagram live to help them get through their difficult days.

Each night, we would have about 30-50 participants playing for $20 gift certificate to the restaurant of their choice. The amazing thing is that most of the winners refused to accept their gift card, and added to it with the request that I give the gift card to someone who needed it worse than them.

After a few weeks of this, I had a collection of a lot of trivia questions. Friends would email me and ask for them so they could use them for a virtual contest with their friends. I was happy to oblige, but then got the idea that I should turn the questions into a book. That book became "Timeless Trivia Volume One." Because of the popularity and success of the initial book, we have now done five more.

A few friends suggested that I write a trivia book for kids. I don't have my own kids, so I thought it would be difficult for me to come up with questions suited for young people. Then I had an idea: " I should have kids write it with me!"

I contacted a few bright relatives and children of friends with the proposition of them helping me with this endeavor. So, many of the questions in this book were written by my young co-authors. (There is a brief biography of each of them in the back.)

We hope that this book, like all of our books, brings you joy, knowledge, and togetherness.

Please help support us at "Timeless Trivia" by writing a review for the book on Amazon and sharing on your social media.

Thanks so much, hope you have a great time!

Yours in Trivia,

Bob Hammitt

1. Which of the 50 United States has the most people?

2. In "Paw Patrol," what is the name of the young boy who leads the crew of rescue dogs upon which the show is based?

3. What was the colorful title of Taylor Swift's 2012 album that included the hit single, "All Too Well"?

4. Which Major League Baseball team has won the most World Series?

5. In the 1989 animated movie "The Little Mermaid," what are the names of Ursula's two evil helpers?

6. In what 1999 movie did Michael J. Fox do the voice of a mouse who was adopted by a family as their middle child?

7. Which popular video game uses a currency known as "V-Bucks?"

Answers

1) California
3) "Red"
5) Flotsam and Jetsam
7) Fortnite

2) Ryder
4) New York Yankees*
6) "Stuart Little"

*As of 2022, the Yankees have won 27 World Series. The Cardinals are second with 11, the Red Sox are third with nine.

8. How many keys are there on a piano?

9. In soccer, how many players play on the field for each team?

10. In the Netflix original movie, "The Secret Life of Pets," what type of an animal is Max?

11. At which of Disneyland's themed lands would you find "Big Thunder Mountain Railroad" and the "Mark Twain Riverboat?"

12. What is the square root of 121?

13. As of 2022, who has the most followers on the social media platform "TikTok"?

14. Who, in 1865, became the first American president ever to be assassinated?

Answers

8) 88   9) 11
10) Dog   11) Frontierland
12) 11   13) Charli D'Amelio
14) Abraham Lincoln*

Four Presidents have been assassinated: Abraham Lincoln, James Garfield, William McKinley, and John F. Kennedy.

15.   Who played the title character in the 2002 film, "Spider-Man"?

16.   What are the names of Harry Potter's parents?

17.   Whose 2020 album "Future Nostalgia" earned six Grammy nominations and included the singles "Physical" and "Break My Heart"?

18.   John Goodman did the voice of James P. Sullivan and Billy Crystal did the same for Mike Wazowski in what 2001 computer-animated Pixar film?

19.   In the movie "Cars," what number is Lightning McQueen's car?

20.   In the game "Yahtzee," how many points is a player awarded for a full house?

21.   What is the name of the crab who serves as an advisor to King Triton in the 1989 film "The Little Mermaid"?

Answers

15) Tobey Maguire*   16) James and Lily
17) Dua Lipa   18) "Monsters, Inc."
19) 95   20) 25
21) Sebastian

*In feature films, Spider-Man has also been played by Tom Holland and Andrew Garfield.

22. What is the only sport to have been played on the moon?

23. What is the last name of the U.S. president after whom Teddy Bears were named?

24. What is the proper word used to refer to a female deer?

25. Rowley Jefferson is the best friend of Greg Heffley in what popular series?

26. Which planet is second-closest to the sun?

27. In the movie and series "The Boss Baby," what is the Boss Baby's older brother's first name?

28. What is the only NFL team in history to go undefeated in the regular season and win the Super Bowl in the same season?

Answers

22) Golf*
24) Doe
26) Venus
28) Miami Dolphins (1972)

23) Roosevelt
25) "Diary of a Wimpy Kid"
27) Timothy or "Tim"

On the Apollo 14th mission in 1971, astronaut Alan Shepard took two shots with his six-iron.

29. The five U.S. Great Lakes are Superior, Erie, Michigan, Huron and what?

30. What is the name of America's (and the world's) oldest national park?

31. Which character of the "Peanuts" gang was often seen with a security blanket?

32. In "The Chronicles of Narnia: The Lion, the Witch, and the Wardrobe" what is the first name of the lion?

33. How many notes are there in an octave?

34. Name the Canadian rapper, actor, and singer who, as of 2022, is the most-streamed artist in the history of Spotify.

35. Name the classic children's bedtime story written by Margaret Wise Brown and illustrated by Clement Hurd which takes readers through the nighttime ritual of saying "goodnight" to everything in the "great green room."

Answers

29) Lake Ontario
31) Linus
33) Eight
35) "Goodnight Moon"

30) Yellowstone
32) Aslan
34) Drake*

Drake is followed by Ed Sheeran at number two, and Eminem is third.

36. What is the name of the second-longest running animated show in the history of Nickelodeon, based on the life of Timmy Turner and his two fairy Godparents.

37. What legendary music performer is often referred to as "The King of Pop"?

38. How many noses does a slug have?

39. Which of Santa Claus's reindeer shares its name with another famous holiday character?

40. Name the popular actress who played the character of Madison in the 2021 film, "Godzilla vs. Kong."

41. In which state is Disneyworld located?

42. As of 2022, what is the highest grossing animated film of all time?

Answers

36) "The Fairly Oddparents" 37) Michael Jackson
38) Four 39) Cupid
40) Millie Bobby Brown 41) Florida
42) "The Lion King" (2019)*

*The 2019 remake of "The Lion King" overtook "Frozen II" for the top spot, which is now second. The original "Frozen" is in third, followed by "The Incredibles 2" and "Minions."

43. What movie features the famous line "Hello, My name is Inigo Montoya. You killed my father. Prepare to die."

44. What is the only number that has the same number of letters as its value?

45. In what 1991 Disney film does a rude, mean, and arrogant hunter named Gaston try to get Belle to marry him?

46. Name the quarterback who played in college at Texas Tech who became the first in history to throw for 5,000 yards in a season in both college and pro football when he did it with the Kansas City Chiefs in the 2018-2019 season.

47. In the American Southwest, there is a famous location known as "Four Corners," where four states touch each other. Those states are Utah, Colorado, Arizona and what?

48. In 1983, Sally Ride became the first American woman to do what?

49. What song, sang by Kermit the Frog, reached No. 25 on the Billboard Top 100 chart in 1979?

Answers

43) "The Princess Bride"
45) "Beauty and the Beast"
47) New Mexico
49) "Rainbow Connection"

44) Four
46) Patrick Mahomes
48) Travel to space*

*In 1963, Valentina Tereshkova of the Soviet Union became the first woman in space. Ride became the first American woman as part of the Space Shuttle Challenger crew.

50. In the popular game "cornhole," how many points are needed to win?

51. What name applies to animals that only eat plants?

52. How many inches are in a yard?

53. What is the name of the ice planet that hosts the first scenes from "Star Wars Episode V: The Empire Strikes Back"?

54. The piccolo, flute, clarinet, and oboe are all considered part of which family of musical instruments?

55. In the 2016 movie "Moana," who plays the voice of the character named Maui?

56. A group of which type of animal is known as a "tower"?

Answers

50) 21
52) 36
54) Woodwinds
56) Giraffes

51) Herbivores*
53) Hoth
55) Dwayne "The Rock" Johnson

*Animals that only eat meat are known as carnivores. Animals that eat both plants and meat are known as omnivores.

57. In 2021, what overtook Google as the most visited website in the world?

58. In 2014, Malala Yousafzai became the youngest person to ever win what highly prestigious award?

59. Which branch of the United States military has the most members?

60. What was the name of the 2018 sequel to the 2012 Disney movie "Wreck-it Ralph?"

61. In 2020, what musician became the first male to appear solo on the cover of Vogue magazine?

62. What popular board game includes "The Rainbow Trail" and "Gumdrop Pass?"

63. In the Harry Potter series, how did the four houses of Hogwarts get their names?

Answers

57) TikTok
58) The Nobel Peace Prize*
59) The Army
60) "Ralph Breaks the Internet"
61) Harry Styles
62) "Candy Land"
63) They are named after the last names of their founders.

Yousafzai won the award at age 17. The previous youngest winner was Dr. Martin Luther King, Jr., who was 35.

64. What is the name of the YouTube star who made $26 million in 2019 at the age of eight?

65. What is the name of the popular animated series on Nickelodeon about the chaotic life of a middle child named Lincoln in a family of 11?

66. Name the 2017 movie about 10-year-old Auggie Pullman, who lives in Brooklyn and deals with the challenges of living with Treacher Collins Syndrome.

67. Name the singer who received an Academy Award nomination for his song "Can't Stop the Feeling" which was featured in the 2016 film "Trolls."

68. What is a scientist who studies plants?

69. In which European country were composers Ludwig Van Beethoven and Johann Sebastian Bach born?

70. In the popular television show "Friends," which character frequently asks "How ya doin'?"

Answers

64) Ryan Kaji*　　　　65) "The Loud House"
66) "Wonder"　　　　67) Justin Timberlake
68) Botanist　　　　69) Germany
70) Joey

*Ryan hosts a YouTube channel called "Ryan's World' with his family in which he reviews toys and tackles other topics. He was the highest earner on YouTube in 2018, 2019, and 2020.

71. Which popular video game series features hostile mobs known as "endermites"?

72. What type of animals are the title characters of the popular 2017 children's book "Boabwaa and Wooliam"?

73. How many miles are in a marathon?

74. BTS became the first K-pop band to be nominated for a Grammy award in 2020. For what song did they receive this nomination?

75. In 1957, Wham-O began selling what popular flying toy named after the owner of a pie company in Connecticut?

76. Name the popular children's show which debuted in 2012 and is based on a character named Daniel and the neighborhood of Make-Believe.

77. What is the only number that is spelled in alphabetical order?

Answers

71) Minecraft   72) Sheep
73) 26.2   74) "Dynamite"
75) The Frisbee*   76) "Daniel Tiger's Neighborhood"
77) Forty

*Teenagers would throw empty pie saucers from the company owned by William Frisbie, yelling "Frisbie" as they flew. Two students took the idea and invented a flying saucer which could travel further, calling it the "Frisbee."

78. Maverick and Goose were two characters who said, "I feel the need.....the need for speed" in which 1986 movie?

79. How many cookies are in a baker's dozen?

80. In which video game series would you find the characters Tom Nook, Mr. Resetti, and K.K. Slider?

81. Which American president famously said, "Ask not what your country can do for you, but what you can do for your country," in 1961?

82. Which popular children's show features characters named Beep, Bing, Bang, Boop, and Bo?

83. Name the Canadian-born singer whose albums include "Handwritten," "Illuminate," and "Wonder."

84. Every April 15, each Major League Baseball team has everyone in uniform wear the number 42. What former player are they honoring by doing this?

Answers

78) "Top Gun"   79) 13
80) "Animal Crossing"   81) John F. Kennedy
82) "Ask the Storybots"   83) Shawn Mendes
84) Jackie Robinson*

*Mr. Robinson was the first African American player to participate in Major League baseball. April 15 is chosen because it was on that date in 1947 on which Robinson broke the color line.

85. Name the 2015 Disney movie in which Kevin Costner stars as the coach of a mostly Latino high school cross country team in California.

86. What is the name of the animated series which began in 2018 about a little girl in Plainfield, Ohio, who loves everything fancy and French?

87. What is the fastest land animal in the world?

88. What is the name of the fictional town in Indiana in which the popular series "Stranger Things" is set?

89. What is a young kangaroo called?

90. What country gave the Statue of Liberty to the United States?

91. In the ballet "The Nutcracker," who is the evil king which the Nutcracker battles?

Answers

85) "McFarland, U.S.A."   86) "Fancy Nancy"
87) Cheetah   88) Hawkins
89) Joey   90) France*
91) The Mouse King

Edouard Rene de Laboulaye, a French scholar, wanted to commemorate the work of the recently deceased Abraham Lincoln, and also to inspire the French people to create their own democracy similar to that of the United States.

92. In 1981, Sandra Day O'Connor became the first woman to serve as what important role in the United States?

93. In the 2008 film "Speed Racer," what is Speed Racer's older brother's name?

94. What is the currency (money) used in the game "Welcome to Bloxburg" called?

95. Which of the earth's seven continents has the most people living on it?

96. Who was the first animated character to have a star on Hollywood's famous "Walk of Fame"?

97. When he becomes angry, which Marvel character does Dr. Bruce Banner become?

98. What is the only mammal that can fly?

Answers

92) Supreme Court Justice   93) Rex Racer
94) Robux   95) Asia*
96) Mickey Mouse   97) The Incredible Hulk
98) Bat

*The continents ranked by population are: 1.Asia, 2. Africa, 3. Europe, 4. North America, 5. South America, 6. Oceania, and 7. Antarctica.

99. What is the name of the popular children's book released in 2021, which is a re-telling of the classic book "The Little Engine That Could?"

100. In the Disney movie "Sleeping Beauty," what are the names of Princess Aurora's fairy godmothers?

101. Which planet has the most moons?

102. On which part of the body are a butterfly's taste buds mostly located?

103. Which character in the Mario Kart series spurts large blots of ink?

104. In the television series "Rugrats," what are the names of the two regular characters that are twins?

105. Who joined Lady Gaga in the duet "Rain on Me," which won the 2021 MTV music award for Song of the Year?

Answers

99) "Three Little Engines"   100) Flora, Fauna, and Merryweather
101) Saturn*   102) Feet
103) Blooper   104) Phil and Lil
105) Ariana Grande

Saturn and Jupiter each have 53 named moons, but Saturn has 29 more that are waiting to be confirmed and named.

106. Name the Manchester United soccer star who as of February 2022 had the most Instagram followers of anyone in the world.

107. In which Marvel movie did S.H.I.E.L.D. agent Phil Coulson make his first appearance?

108. What video game, featuring travel through the mushroom kingdom, was first released in 1985?

109. In the movie "The Little Mermaid," what type of utensil is "The Dinglehopper?"

110. In what 2010 animated movie would you find characters named Hiccup, Gobber, and Fishlegs Ingerman?

111. Giant pandas get 99 percent of all their food from what type of plant?

112. In the popular animated comedy "The Amazing World of Gumball," what type of animal is Gumball?

Answers

106) Cristiano Ronaldo
108) Super Mario Bros
110) "How to Train Your Dragon"
112) A cat

107) "Iron Man"
109) A fork
111) Bamboo

Ronaldo has 453 million followers. The remaining top five are Lionel Messi, Kylie Jenner, Ariana Grande, and Dwayne "The Rock" Johnson.

113. At what age can a person legally vote in the United States?

114. In the popular video game "Minecraft," what are the hostile mobs which sneak up on players before they explode?

115. In the movie "Frozen," how many brothers does Prince Hans have?

116. In "The Lion King," what is the name of Simba's father?

117. What was the most streamed song on Spotify in the year 2020?

118. How many valves are found in the human heart?

119. In the 2021 movie "Clifford the Big Red Dog," what is the name of Clifford's owner and human friend?

Answers

113) 18   114) Creepers
115) 12   116) Mufasa
117) "Blinding Lights"*   118) Four
119) Emily Elizabeth

* "Blinding Lights" by the Weeknd was No. 1. The remainder of the top five were "Roses" by SAINt JHN, "Rockstar" by DaBaby, "The Box" by Roddy Rich, and "Dance Monkey" by Tones and I.

120. What does the Roman number "X" equal?

121. In the 2018 movie "Ready Player One," what is the real name of the main character who goes by the avatar name "Parzival"?

122. What are the arcs called which are created by light striking water droplets?

123. What is the capital of France?

124. What is the name of the popular British band that is led by vocalist Chris Martin?

125. According to Babycenter, what was the most popular name for newborn females in the United States in 2021?

126. In the board game "Sorry," what must a player do if they draw a card with the number four on it?

Answers

120) Ten
122) Rainbows
124) Coldplay
126) Move back four spaces

121) Wade Watts
123) Paris
125) Olivia*

After Olivia are the names Emma, Amelia, Ava, and Sophia.

127. In the popular nursery rhyme "Jack and Jill," what did Jack break when he fell?

128. What team NFL football did legend John Madden coach to a Super Bowl victory?

129. Blinky, Inky, Clyde and Pinky are all characters in which classic video game?

130. What is a female donkey called?

131. What are the names of Cinderella's step-sisters?

132. In which city was the Declaration of Independence signed?

133. In a popular book series, who is Annabeth Chase's boyfriend?

Answers

127) His crown

128) The Oakland Raiders

129) Pacman

130) A Jenny

131) Anastasia and Drizella

132) Philadelphia

133) Percy Jackson*

Percy and Annabeth are both Greek Demigods in the series "Percy Jackson and the Olympians."

134. Using the Celsius system of measurement, at what temperature does water freeze?

135. Which holiday is celebrated in America on the fourth Thursday of each November?

136. In the 1992 film "Home Alone 2," in which city does Kevin get separated from his family?

137. What category of trees shed their leaves every year?

138. If you add ¼ of a cup of sugar to ¼ of a cup of sugar, what fraction of a cup of sugar do you now have?

139. In the 2005 movie "Madagascar," what is the name of the Zebra who desires a life outside of the zoo?

140. What is the name of the 2016 film in which a theater owner named Buster Moon holds a singing competition to try to save his struggling theater?

Answers

134) Zero degrees   135) Thanksgiving*
136) New York   137) Deciduous
138) ½   139) Marty
140) "Sing"

President George Washington was the first to proclaim Thanksgiving a national celebration, and President Abraham Lincoln made it an annual holiday in all states, but it was not set to a fixed day until 1941 by President Franklin D. Roosevelt.

141. In the popular Nickelodeon series "Zoey 101," what is the name of Zoey's brother?

142. In the 1985 movie "Back to the Future," what year does Marty McFly go back to?

143. In the Netflix original series "Octonauts: Above and Beyond" what is the name of the brave polar bear who serves as the captain of the Octonauts?

144. What is a shape with eight sides called?

145. What do most female octopuses do about the same time that their eggs hatch?

146. In the 2000 movie "The Emperor's New Groove," what type of animal does Emperor Kuzco turn into?

147. What is the largest state in America?

Answers

141) Dustin   142) 1985
143) Barnacles   144) Octagon
145) Die*   146) A llama
147) Alaska

*The female octopus stops eating after laying her eggs. Her last few days are spent caring for the eggs, and she usually expires right around the time they hatch.

148. What is the name of the boy who explores his neighborhood after the season's first snowfall in the 1962 classic children's book, "The Snowy Day"?

149. In the Marvel comic series, what is Pepper Potts allergic to?

150. Which amendment to the United States Constitution protects freedom of speech?

151. What is the name of the hunter who is a longtime enemy of Bugs Bunny?

152. What is the only bird that can fly backwards and upside down?

153. In auto racing, what type of flag is waved when someone has won the race?

154. What is the name of the monkey who is Dora the Explorer's best friend?

Answers

148) Peter
149) Strawberries
150) The First*
151) Elmer Fudd
152) Hummingbird
153) Checkered flag
154) Boots

*The First Amendment also protects separation of church and state, freedom of religion, freedom of the press, the right to assemble, and the right to petition the government.

155. What is a group of whales called?

156. In the 2013 movie "Despicable Me 2," who sings the song "Happy"?

157. In what country did the Olympic games originate?

158. In the movie "The Jungle Book," what type of animal is the character Baloo?

159. In the 2005 film "Charlie and the Chocolate Factory," how many golden tickets have been placed in Wonka Bars?

160. According to Billboard Magazine, what song by Dua Lipa was the No. 1 song of 2021?

161. In the hit Nickelodeon series "Icarly," in what city does Carly live?

Answers

155) A pod
157) Greece
159) Five
161) Seattle

156) Pharrell Williams
158) A bear
160) "Levitating"*

*This is the first time that a female has had the No. 1 song in ten years, with the previous time being Adele's "Rolling in the Deep" in 2011.

162. In the 1996 movie "101 Dalmatians," what is the name of Roger Dearly's pet Dalmatian?

163. What is the largest species of bird in the world?

164. What is the name of the Italian artist who painted "The Mona Lisa?"

165. Harvard, Yale, Cornell, Princeton, and Brown Universities all belong to what league?

166. What is the name of the rabbit who becomes a police officer in the 2016 movie "Zootopia"?

167. Helsinki is the capital city of which country?

168. In what city is the 2009 film "The Princess and the Frog" set?

Answers

162) Pongo
164) Leonardo da Vinci
166) Judy Hopps
168) New Orleans

163) Ostrich*
165) The Ivy League
167) Finland

*An ostrich can be more than nine feet tall, weigh more than 300 pounds, and run at speeds greater than 40 mph!

169. What is the name of the popular Nickelodeon series about the adventures of 13-year-old Henry Hart, who lives in the town of Swellview?

170. Name the female rapper who won the Grammy for best new artist at the 2021 award show, whose debut album in 2020 was titled "Good News."

171. What candy's slogan is "Taste the Rainbow"?

172. What is the only insect that can turn its head?

173. In what state were the first shots of the American Revolution fired?

174. In the Marvel comic series, what is the name of the doctor who protects the earth from magical and mystical threats?

175. What is the name of the 2010 Disney film which tells the story of Rapunzel, a young princess with magical hair?

Answers

169) "Henry Danger"
171) Skittles
173) Massachusetts
175) "Tangled"

170) Megan Thee Stallion
172) Praying Mantis*
174) Dr. Strange

*House flies can tilt their head very slightly, but a praying mantis can turn its head 180 degrees. They also have excellent eyesight, being able to see clearly more than fifty feet away.

176. How many milliliters are in one liter?

177. Name the actor who played the lead role of Troy Bolton in the 2006 movie "High School Musical."

178. What is the name of the volcano in Washington that erupted in 1980?

179. In the television series "Sesame Street," what is the name of Big Bird's best friend?

180. Which of the 50 United States was the last to join the union?

181. Who hosted a famous show about science on PBS from 1993 to 1998?

182. Wellington is the capital city of which country?

Answers

176) 1,000
178) Mount Saint Helens*
180) Hawaii
182) New Zealand

177) Zac Efron
179) Snuffy
181) Bill Nye

Mount Saint Helens is the most recently active volcano in the continental United States, the last one to erupt was Mt. Lassen in northern California in 1915.

183. What is the title of the 2020 Netflix children's movie about an inventor named Jeronicus who builds a magical toy that comes to life?

184. What is name of the trophy given to each year's champions of the National Hockey League?

185. On which continent have the most dinosaur fossils been found?

186. What country music singer appeared with Lil Nas X on the popular 2019 remix of his song "Old Town Road"?

187. What is the name of the red haired, yodeling cowgirl who makes her first appearance in "Toy Story 2"?

188. Manx cats are unique because they often lack which physical feature?

189. In the animated series "Doug," what is the name of the girl that Doug has a crush on?

Answers

183) "Jingle Jangle: A Christmas Journey"   184) The Stanley Cup
185) North America   186) Billy Ray Cyrus
187) Jessie   188) Tail*
189) Patti Mayonnaise

*Manx cats are from the Isle of Man, in the Irish sea. Some have stubs, but many are completely tail-less.

190. What is the most populated country in the world?

191. Who is the only Disney princess with a tattoo?

192. What is the name of the character played by Harrison Ford in the original "Star Wars" films?

193. In the popular animated series "Peppa Pig," what is Peppa's younger brother's name?

194. Which state is nicknamed "The Sunshine State?"

195. How many strings do most guitars have?

196. What is the name of the town where Spongebob Squarepants lives?

Answers

190) China

191) Pocahontas*

192) Han Solo

193) George

194) Florida

195) Six

196) Bikini Bottom

Pocahontas is also the only Disney princess to be based on a real person.

197. What is the name of the TV series which originally aired on the Disney Channel from 2002 to 2007 about a crime fighting high school female in Middleton, USA?

198. Which western university has a mascot known as "Benny the Beaver?"

199. What is the largest land animal in the world?

200. Which European country is home to a Disney theme park?

201. How often do years with an extra day, known as "leap years," occur?

202. How many points are awarded in football for a "safety"?

203. In "The Wizard of Oz," what is the first name of the good witch, from the south?

Answers

197) "Kim Possible"
199) The African elephant
201) Every four years
203) Glinda

198) Oregon State University
200) France*
202) Two

*There are two in the United States, one in China, one in Hong Kong, one in Japan, and one in Paris, France.

204. Between which two planets is the asteroid belt located?

205. In the 2002 movie "Ice Age," what type of animal is Scrat?

206. Who played the title character in the 2018 film "Christopher Robin"?

207. Who won the CMA award for best entertainer of 2021, based in part for his album titled "What You See is What You Get"?

208. What is the fastest land animal in the western hemisphere?

209. What company was founded in Denmark in 1934 whose name is the combination of the Danish words for "play well?"

210. What event is a track and field competition includes ten different athletic events?

Answers

204) Mars and Jupiter
206) Ewan McGregor
208) Antelope
210) Decathlon*

205) Squirrel
207) Luke Combs
209) Lego

The ten events for the decathlon are: 100-meter dash, long jump, shot put, high jump, 400-meter run, 110-meter hurdles, discus, pole vault, javelin, and 1500-meter run.

211. If it is winter in the Northern Hemisphere, what season is it in the Southern Hemisphere?

212. What is the name of the girl who flies off to Neverland with Peter Pan?

213. What is the name of the 1995 movie starring Robin Williams about a man from a board game brought into the real world?

214. At what U.S. national park was the record set for hottest temperature ever recorded in the United States?

215. What is the proper math term for an angle which is less than 90 degrees?

216. What game, released by Milton Bradley in 1966, uses the slogan "The game that ties you up in knots?"

217. What is the only fruit with its seeds on the outside?

Answers

211) Summer
213) "Jumanji"
215) Acute
217) Strawberry

212) Wendy Darling
214) Death Valley*
216) Twister

*In 1913, a temperature of 134 degrees was recorded at Death Valley's Furnace Creek.

218. What is the name of the 2010 movie in which a boy named "Hiccup" captures and becomes friends with a creature named "Night Fury"?

219. How many movies are there in "The Santa Clause" series, starring Tim Allen as Santa?

220. What has the longest pregnancy of any living mammal?

221. Which state is known as both "The North Star State" and "The Land of 10,000 lakes"?

222. What are the names of Donald Duck's three nephews?

223. Which of Snow White's seven dwarves always wears a purple cap, and is the only one without a beard?

224. What is the name of the NFL team which is based in New Orleans, Louisiana?

Answers

218) "How to Train Your Dragon"   219) Three
220) Elephants*   221) Minnesota
222) Huey, Dewey, and Louie   223) Dopey
224) The Saints

*The average pregnancy of an elephant lasts 18-22 months.

225. In the 2015 movie titled "Inside Out," to what city do Riley and her parents move?

226. Mt. Everest is the highest mountain in the world. It is part of what mountain range?

227. What is the best-selling PlayStation game of all time?

228. From what country are the popular children's musical group "The Wiggles"?

229. How many players are on the court per team in the sport of volleyball?

230. In the popular book and television series "Arthur," what kind of an animal is Arthur?

231. What is the name of the official currency (money) of Japan?

Answers

225) San Francisco
227) Gran Turismo*
229) Six
231) Yen

226) The Himalayas
228) Australia
230) Aardvark

Gran Turismo has sold about 11 million copies. Rounding out the top five are Final Fantasy VII, Gran Turismo 2, Final Fantasy VIII, and Tekken 3.

232. The three-toed sloth holds the title of _____ mammal in the world.

233. What is the name of the 1997 Disney animated film based on a son of the Greek god Zeus?

234. Which U.S. state has the most miles of coastline?

235. What is the last name of the famous TikTok star known as "Baby Ariel"?

236. What is the name of Harry Potter's pet owl?

237. Name the American swimmer who has won more Olympic gold medals than any other person in history.

238. What 1998 Pixar movie features a grasshopper named "Hopper" and Ants named "Flik" and "Dot"?

Answers

232) Slowest
234) Alaska
236) Hedwig
238) "A Bug's Life"

233) "Hercules"
235) Martin
237) Michael Phelps*

*Phelps has won 23 gold medals. He has won 28 overall, which is also a record.

239. In Dr. Seuss's book "The Cat in the Hat," whose house does the cat visit?

240. Name the country music singers who won the Grammy award for Best Country Duo/Group performance in 2019, 2020, and 2021.

241. What is the name of the 2017 film about a 12-year-old boy named Miguel, who is accidentally transported to the land of the dead?

242. Which country produces more coffee than any other in the world?

243. What is the bottom number in a fraction known as?

244. What is the name of Popeye's girlfriend?

245. Which American city is often referred to as "The Motor City" because of the many cars that have been built there?

Answers

239) Sally

240) Dan + Shay

241) "Coco"

242) Brazil*

243) Denominator

244) Olive Oyl

245) Detroit, Michigan

*The next most producing coffee countries are Vietnam, Columbia, Indonesia, and Ethiopia.

246.   In the book "Curious George," what color hat is the man who captures George wearing?

247.   What is the name of the man who turns into "Captain America?"

248.   How many eyes do caterpillars have?

249.   Name the singer whose hits include "Uptown Funk," "Marry You," and "24K Magic."

250.   What is the name of the Disney Channel sitcom which centered on the life of a character named Alex Russo, who was played by Selena Gomez?

251.   Which planet is brightest in the Earth's night sky?

252.   How many pints are in a quart?

Answers

246) Yellow   247) Steve Rogers
248) 12   249) Bruno Mars
250) "Wizards of Waverly Place"   251) Venus
252) Two

*Venus shines brightly because it is the closest planet to Earth, and it is surrounded with a thick layer of clouds which reflect the sunlight.

253. In the 1964 movie "Mary Poppins," what does Mary suggest helps the medicine go down?

254. In the Wii version of Mario Kart, what is the name of the final racetrack?

255. What, made by humans, connects the Atlantic and Pacific Oceans?

256. Name the animated movie and television series based on an aspiring scientist named Flint, his father Tim, and a monkey assistant named Steve.

257. Which part of the cell is often referred to as "the powerhouse of the cell?"

258. What is the name of the rapper who is married to Beyoncé?

259. Name the game in which players compete by removing things from a person such as their "Wish Bone," "Bread Basket," and "Charley Horse."

Answers

253) A spoonful of sugar   254) Rainbow Road
255) The Panama Canal   256) "Cloudy With a Chance of Meatballs"
257) Mitochondria   258) Jay-Z
259) Operation*

*Operation was designed by a student at the University of Illinois as part of a class project.

260. In the 1996 film "Matilda," what is Matilda's last name?

261. How many legs do all insects have?

262. In Chapter One of "Alice's Adventures in Wonderland," Alice falls down what type of hole?

263. What popular video game is based on the challenges faced by a courageous young Hylian man named Link?

264. What sea creatures travel in groups called "pods" and sleep with one eye open?

265. As of 2022, which two NFL teams are tied for the most Super Bowl victories?

266. In the movie "Aladdin," what does Aladdin search for in the Cave of Wonders?

Answers

260) Wormwood
262) Rabbit hole
264) Dolphins
266) A magic lamp

261) Six
263) "The Legend of Zelda"
265) The New England Patriots and Pittsburgh Steelers*

*The Steelers and Patriots have each won six. The Cowboys and 49ers have the next most with five each.

267. What is the first name of the star panda in the movie "Kung Fu Panda"?

268. How many people serve on the United States Supreme Court?

269. What is the fraction 22/7 commonly referred to as in math?

270. What is the name of the Disney channel drama about a 12-year-old who moves into a haunted town in Louisiana which debuted in 2021?

271. In what state would you find the Grand Canyon?

272. Who is the oldest Jonas brother?

273. Although she was born with the name Melissa Viviane Jefferson, what is the singer and rapper whose hits include "Juice" and "Tempo" better known as?

Answers

267) Po
269) Pi*
271) Arizona
273) Lizzo

268) Nine
270) "Secrets of Sulphur Springs"
272) Kevin

*Pi is the relationship between a circle's circumference to its diameter.

274. In "Finding Nemo," how old is Crush?

275. What is the most populated city in the world?

276. Which state is known as "The Lone Star State?"

277. From which part of the body does a dog sweat?

278. What fruit do raisins come from?

279. What fast food restaurant uses the slogan "Have it Your Way?"

280. What kind of a dog is "Snoopy?"

Answers

274) 150 years
276) Texas
278) Grapes
280) Beagle

275) Tokyo, Japan*
277) Paws
279) Burger King

*Tokyo is followed by Delhi, India, Shanghai, China, Sao Paulo, Brazil, and Mexico City, Mexico.

281. How many inches are in a yard?

282. What 2008 Pixar movie is about two robots who fall in love while trying to save the world?

283. Who was the first African-American player to play Major League Baseball?

284. In the movie "Mulan," what is the name of Mulan's dragon?

285. Whose song "Driver's License" broke the Spotify record for most streams in a single day for a non-holiday song in 2021?

286. Whose picture is on the ten dollar bill?

287. In which country is the movie "The Jungle Book" set?

Answers

281) 36

282) "Wall-E"

283) Jackie Robinson

284) Mushu

285) Olivia Rodrigo*

286) Alexander Hamilton

287) India

*Rodrigo's record for most streams in a day was broken in October, 2021, by Adele's song "Easy On Me."

288. What type of science is defined as the study of all living things?

289. On what popular children's television show did Miranda Cosgrove star as Megan Parker from 2004 to 2007?

290. What is the name of the astronaut who in 1969 became the first person ever to walk on the moon?

291. The popular board game "Chutes and Ladders" was originally called "_____ and Ladders."

292. What is a group of fish called?

293. What is a polygon with six sides known as?

294. What is the name of the 2015 Pixar movie about the emotions of joy, sadness, fear, anger, and disgust as people?

Answers

288) Biology
290) Neil Armstrong
292) A school
294) "Inside Out"

289) "Drake and Josh"
291) Snakes
293) Hexagon

*"Snakes and Ladders" originated in ancient India. It became popular in the United Kingdom in the 1890s. The Milton Bradley company changed the game to become "Chutes and Ladders" in 1943.

295. In what state did the American Revolution begin?

296. Copenhagen is the capital city of which country?

297. What is a Smurf's house shaped like?

298. What species of bird is the smallest in the world?

299. What type of animal is the popular children's cartoon legend named Pororo?

300. What film, released in 2020, has made the most money of any film based upon a video game in history?

301. In bowling, what score is considered a "perfect game"?

Answers

295) Massachusetts   296) Denmark
297) Mushroom   298) Hummingbird
299) Penguin   300) Sonic the Hedgehog
301) 300*

*Two achieve a 300 game, a player must bowl 12 consecutive strikes.

302. Which part of a cat is as unique as a human fingerprint?

303. Name the popular singer who has released four albums which use math symbols as their titles.

304. In terms of total square miles, what is the largest country in the world?

305. What is the name of the alter ego of the popular comic book character "Iron Man"?

306. In "The Muppet Show," what are the names of the two old men characters who sit above the stage and heckle?

307. What planet has a red spot which is more than 10,000 miles wide?

308. Which animals hold hands while they sleep in water?

Answers

302) Nose*
304) Russia
306) Statler and Waldorf
308) Otters

303) Ed Sheeran
305) Tony Stark
307) Jupiter

*A cat's nose has a unique series of ridges on it, just like the human finger.

309. In the sentence "Larry ran quickly to the store," which word is the adverb?

310. A video of what children's song became the first YouTube video to reach 10 billion views in January, 2022?

311. Not counting tomato sauce or cheese, what is the most commonly used pizza topping in the world?

312. What is the name of the oldest tennis tournament in the world, which is held in England every summer?

313. What is the motto of the Boy Scouts?

314. What is the name of the popular video game released in 2015 which is described as "soccer, but with rocket powered cars?"

315. In which classic fairy tale does a miller lie to a king, telling him that his daughter can spin straw into gold?

Answers

309) Quickly
311) Pepperoni*
313) Be Prepared
315) "Rumpelstiltskin"

310) "Baby Shark Dance"
312) Wimbledon
314) "Rocket League"

Following pepperoni as the most popular pizza toppings in the world are mushrooms, extra cheese, sausage, onions and black olives.

316. Which two countries share the longest border in the world?

317. Name the popular children's show which is based on a club for children known as "The Squirrel Club."

318. What is the name of the popular YouTube series created by Dane Boedigheimer about a fruit who tells jokes and puns about other fruits.

319. Into which ocean does the Amazon River flow?

320. In the 2009 film "Fantastic Mr. Fox", what is Mr. Fox's wife's name?

321. Old Mother Hubbard went to the cupboard to give the poor dog a what?

322. How many minutes are in seven hours?

Answers

316) The United States and Canada* 317) "Hey Duggee"
318) "Annoying Orange"   319) Atlantic Ocean
320) Felicity   321) Bone
322) 420

The second longest border is between Russia and Kazakhstan, the third is between Argentina and Chile.

323. What is the name of the popular band from Seattle made up of former elementary school teachers whose albums include "Welcome to Monkey Town," "Hot Air," and "Novelties?"

324. What famous building is located at 1600 Pennsylvania Avenue?

325. What is the name of the series which aired on Nickelodeon from 2003 to 2008 about the characters from "Rugrats" when they got older?

326. Mario Lemieux is a member of the Hall of Fame of which sport?

327. How many teeth do adults have?

328. In the movie "The Emperor's New Groove," what type of animal is Yzma?

329. What community in Pennsylvania is home to one of the world's most popular makers of chocolate?

Answers

323) Recess Monkey   324) The White House
325) "All Grown Up!"   326) Hockey
327) 32328) Cat
329) Hershey*

*Hershey is not officially a town or city, but has 14,000 people who live in it. It was founded by Milton Hershey, who also founded the famous chocolate company.

330. What is the smallest breed of dog in the world?

331. On the popular show "The Adventures of Jimmy Neutron, Boy Genius," what are the names of Jimmy's two best friends?

332. What is the name of the instrument that a doctor uses to listen to a patient's heart beat?

333. What bird has the longest wingspan?

334. What is the name of the 2008 movie about a white shepherd dog who is adopted by a girl named Penny and who also believes he has superpowers?

335. What two singers released the song "I Don't Care" together in 2019, which was a No. 1 single in 26 countries?

336. In "Beauty and the Beast," what is the name of Belle's father?

Answers

330) Chihuahua

331) Sheen and Carl

332) Stethoscope

333) Albatross*

334) "Bolt"

335) Justin Bieber and Ed Sheeran

336) Maurice

*The wandering albatross has the longest wingspan of any albatross, sometimes more than 12 feet.

337. What does the Roman numeral "C" represent?

338. In the movie "Toy Story," what is the name of the piggy bank?

339. When listed alphabetically, which state comes first?

340. What color is a giraffe's tongue?

341. What is the alias of Peter Quill in the Marvel Cinematic Universe series?

342. What is the name of the street that Harry Potter lives on?

343. What actress performed as the voice of Rapunzel in the 2010 movie "Tangled?"

Answers

337) 100
339) Alabama
341) Star-Lord
343) Mandy Moore

338) Hamm
340) Black
342) Privet Drive*

*The house originally used for filming is about 40 miles west of London. It was only used for the first film, as a replica house was built in Hollywood.

344. The kiwi is the national bird of what country?

345. What is the name of the carpenter who created Pinocchio?

346. What is the name of the snake in "The Jungle Book?"

347. What is the name of the galaxy in which the Earth is located?

348. What is the proper term for an animal which can live successfully in both land and water?

349. What is the name of the popular television series in which Miss Frizzle embarks in a vehicle on adventures with her students?

350. In what country can you find the most species of trees?

Answers

344) New Zealand   345) Geppetto
346) Kaa   347) The Milky Way
348) Amphibian   349) "The Magic School Bus"
350) Brazil*

Brazil has more than 8,700 species of trees. Columbia has the second most, Indonesia the third.

351. What is the best-selling Christmas song of all time?

352. What letter does every odd number have in it?

353. In the 2009 film "Up," what is the name of the talking dog?

354. In baseball, what do the letters RBI mean?

355. What is the name of the van in "Scooby Doo"?

356. Which popular fast food restaurant once used the famous slogan, "Where's the Beef?"

357. What is the name of the dragon in the 2016 movie "Pete's Dragon?"

Answers

351) "White Christmas"*   352) E
353) "Dug"   354) Run Batted In
355) "The Mystery Machine"   356) Wendy's
357) Elliot

*With an estimated 50 million copies sold, "White Christmas" is not only the top selling Christmas song, but the top selling song of all time.

358. What country borders both Portugal and France?

359. In the classic cartoon "The Flintstones," what is the name of Fred and Wilma's daughter?

360. What 2021 Disney film features triplet children named Julieta, Pepa, and Bruno?

361. In which ocean is the Bermuda Triangle located?

362. Name the Scottish singer who had a No. 1 hit in 2019 with the song "Someone You Loved."

363. What is the top number in a fraction known as?

364. What American gymnast was named Time Magazine's "Athlete of the Year" in 2021?

Answers

358) Spain
360) "Encanto"
362) Lewis Capaldi
364) Simone Biles*

359) Pebbles
361) Atlantic
363) Numerator

*Biles has many accolades, including most world medals with 25 and most world gold medals with 19. Her seven Olympic medals tie her for the most by a female gymnast in American history.

365. What is the longest river in Africa?

366. What bird has been a national symbol of the United States since 1782?

367. In what film does Mickey Mouse have a teacher named Yen Sid?

368. What is the largest land mammal native to North America?

369. In "The Incredibles," what is the name of the town that Bob and Helen Parr live in with their children Violet, Dash, and baby Jack-Jack?

370. The patella is located at the front of what body part?

371. Dr. James Naismith is credited with inventing which sport?

Answers

365) The Nile
367) "Fantasia"
369) Metroville
371) Basketball

366) The bald eagle
368) The bison*
370) Knee

*In 2016, President Obama signed an act which made the North American Bison the official mammal of the United States.

372. In "The Little Mermaid," how many children does King Triton have?

373. What is the name of the pig saved by a girl named Fern in "Charlotte's Web?"

374. What are leaves which we use to flavor food known as?

375. What is the name of the animated series on Nickelodeon about a boy with supernatural powers who fights ghosts with the help of his best friends Sam Manson and Tucker Foley?

376. What makes up the horns of a rhinoceros?

377. What is the name of the 2007 animated movie about Remy, a rat who is interested in cooking?

378. What is the official national language of Brazil?

Answers

372) Seven

373) Wilbur

374) Herbs

375) "Danny Phantom"

376) Hair*

377) "Ratatouille"

378) Portuguese

*The word "rhinoceros" comes from the Greek words for nose (rhino) and hair (ceros).

379. In what year was the popular game "Pokemon Go" released?

380. Using the Celsius system, at what temperature does water boil?

381. Hale-Bopp, Halley's, Chiron, and Biela's are all names of what type of outer space objects?

382. In the movie "Avatar," what is the name of the former Marine who becomes part of the Avatar program after his twin brother is killed?

383. What three numbers have the same result when you multiply them as when you add them together?

384. What is the name of Shrek's wife?

385. In Dr. Seuss's "The Cat in the Hat," what type of pet does Sally have?

Answers

379) 2016
380) 100 degrees*
381) Comets
382) Jake Sully
383) One, two, and three
384) Fiona
385) A fish

* In the Fahrenheit system, water boils at 212 degrees.

386. What sea creature is the favorite food of baleen whales?

387. What is the name of the elf played by Will Ferrell in the movie "Elf?"

388. In what sport would you find a player known as "The Libero"?

389. What American city is known as the birthplace of jazz and hosts an annual large celebration known as "Mardi Gras?"

390. In what state can you find Mount Rushmore?

391. What are the first names of the Three Chipmunks?

392. Which popular television show features an ice cream parlor named "Scoops Ahoy?"

Answers

386) Krill*
388) Volleyball
390) South Dakota
392) "Stranger Things"

387) Buddy
389) New Orleans, Louisiana
391) Simon, Alvin, Theodore

*Baleen whales include blue whales, fin whales, grey whales, and humpback whales. They may eat other things, like crustaceans, but their diet consists mainly of krill. The blue whale sometimes eats up to four tons of krill in a day.

393. Which holiday is observed in the United States on the last Monday of May each year?

394. Name the female country music singer whose hits include "The Middle," "Girl," and "My Church."

395. In the movie "Spy Kids 3D: Game Over," what is the name of the character who is captured by the Toymaker?

396. How many arms does a sea star have?

397. In what country would you find the Great Barrier Reef?

398. What is the name of the main character in the Nickelodeon series "Avatar: The Last Airbender"?

399. What do you call animals who are active during the night and sleep during the day?

Answers

393) Memorial Day*   394) Maren Morris
395) Carmen   396) Five
397) Australia   398) Aang
399) Nocturnal

*Memorial Day honors the men and women who have died while in service of the United States military. It was first observed in 1868.

400. Which Muppet was known for telling bad jokes?

401. Which American city is known as "The City of Brotherly Love"?

402. What is the last name of the "Peanuts" character named Lucy?

403. What sea creature has no brain, no heart, no blood, and despite its name is not even really a fish?

404. What is the name of the 1992 movie in which an attorney named Gordon Bombay fulfills his sentence for community service by coaching a youth hockey team?

405. How many vowels are there in the English language?

406. What does the "D.C." in Washington, D.C., stand for?

Answers

400) Fozzie
402) Van Pelt*
404) "The Mighty Ducks"
406) District of Columbia

401) Philadelphia
403) Jellyfish
405) Five

*Lucy was named after Louanne Van Pelt, a neighbor of Peanuts creator Charles Schulz, in Colorado Springs, Colorado.

407.   What is a female fox called?

408.   In the Disney series "Diary of a Future President," what is the name of the 13-year-old girl who aspires to be the president of the United States in her future?

409.   Cirrus, Stratus, Cirrocumulus, and Altocumulus are all types of what?

410.   In "Finding Nemo," what is Nemo's mom's name?

411.   What is the term used to describe plants or trees that keep their leaves throughout the year?

412.   Which classic cartoon character repeatedly uses the line "I tawt I taw a puddy tat"?

413.   What type of fish is eaten by humans more than any other in the world?

Answers

407) Vixen   408) Elena
409) Clouds   410) Coral
411) Evergreen   412) Tweety
413) Tuna*

*In second place is salmon, third is cod, fourth is tilapia, and fifth are sardines.

414. What does the acronym "SMH" stand for in texting slang?

415. What is the name of child Instagram star Alexis Olympia Ohanian's famous mother?

416. In the movie "Paddington," in the jungles of what country does a British geographer discover a previously unknown species of bear?

417. Bruce Wayne is the real name of what famous superhero?

418. Which athletic conference do U.C.L.A., U.S.C., and Stanford University belong to?

419. What color is a product of mixing red and yellow together?

420. Which continent contains the most countries?

Answers

414) Shaking my head   415) Serena Williams
416) Peru   417) Batman
418) The Pac-12   419) Orange
420) Africa*

*As of February, 2022: Africa has 54 countries. Europe, with 51, has the second most. Asia is third with 50.

421. What part of our solar system used to be considered a planet but was reclassified to a "dwarf planet" in 2006?

422. What animated show follows the adventures of three Kindergarten girls named Blossom, Bubbles, and Buttercup?

423. In what country would you find the famous statue known as "The Sphinx"?

424. What is the name of the famous museum in France in which you would find the painting titled "The Mona Lisa"?

425. What is the longest running children's television show in American history?

426. What Disney channel show features the characters Luz Noceda, Eda Clawthorne, Willow Park, and Hooty?

427. If there are two or three players participating in the game "Go Fish," how many cards are dealt to each player to begin the game?

Answers

421) Pluto
422) "Powerpuff Girls"
423) Egypt
424) The Louvre
425) "Sesame Street"*
426) "The Owl House"
427) Seven

*"Sesame Street" began airing in 1969. The second-longest running children's show in American history is "Mr. Rogers' Neighborhood," which aired for 31 seasons.

428. What Nickelodeon show, which originally aired from 1994 to 2005, led to the spin-offs "Kenan and Kel," "The Amanda Show," and "The Nick Cannon Show"?

429. H_2O is the chemical symbol for what?

430. What is the first name of the youngest son of Prince Charles and Princess Diana?

431. In the original "Avengers" movie, how many Avengers are there?

432. In the nursery rhyme "The Three Little Kittens," what did the kittens lose?

433. What 2010 movie was the first animated film to make one billion dollars worldwide?

434. What is a male duck known as?

Answers

428) "All That"
430) Harry
432) Their mittens
434) A drake

429) Water
431) Six*
433) "Toy Story 3"

The original Avengers were Iron Man, Captain America, Hulk, Thor, Hawkeye, and Black Widow.

435. In "Snow White and the Seven Dwarves," what time do the dwarves quit work?

436. How many colors are there in a rainbow?

437. In the movie "Aladdin," what kind of animal was Abu?

438. What is the world's largest mammal?

439. How many legs does a lobster have?

440. What is the name of Mickey Mouse's pet dog?

441. Arachnophobia is a term used to describe fear of what?

Answers

435) Five p.m.
437) Monkey
439) Ten
441) Spiders

436) Seven*
438) The blue whale
440) Pluto

The colors of a rainbow are red, orange, green, blue, indigo, violet, and yellow.

442. What is the name of the classic family game in which players try to make words out of lettered dice joining together?

443. What is the name of the 2020 Disney film in which Ian and Barley Lightfoot set out on a quest to find a way to bring their dead father back to life for one more day?

444. What color hat does "Bob the Builder" wear?

445. What Disney movie features the song "Circle of Life?"

446. What is the name of the first American ever to orbit the Earth?

447. On what part of a fish can its caudal fin be found?

448. Name the 1963 children's book, later turned into a movie, about a boy named Max whose bedroom turns into a jungle?

Answers

442) Boggle
444) Yellow
446) John Glenn
448) "Where the Wild Things Are"

443) "Onward"*
445) "The Lion King"
447) The tail

*"Onward" struggled at the box office, because it was released at the beginning of the Covid-19 pandemic. It is considered Pixar's second box office failure, with the other being "The Good Dinosaur."

449. What major organ removes toxins from the body's blood supply?

450. How many holes are played in a full round of golf?

451. What 1993 film tells the story of a boy named Scottie Smalls trying to make friends in a new hometown?

452. How many days are there in a year?

453. In the "Diary of a Wimpy Kid" series, who is Greg's brother?

454. What is the smallest state in America?

455. In the film "The Little Mermaid," what is the name of the boy who Ariel falls in love with?

Answers

449) The liver
451) "The Sandlot"
453) Rodrick
455) Prince Eric

450) 18
452) 365
454) Rhode Island*

*After Rhode Island, the next smallest states are Delaware, Connecticut, Hawaii, and New Jersey.

456. How many zeroes are in a million?

457. In the movie "Tangled," what is the name of Rapunzel's horse?

458. In "The Tale of Peter Rabbit," what is the name of the man whose vegetable garden Peter goes into?

459. Who replaced Franklin D. Roosevelt as President of the United States?

460. Oxygen and nutrients are transported in human blood by what color cells?

461. In "The Wizard of Oz," what is the name of Dorothy's dog?

462. Which country has won the most men's World Cups in soccer?

Answers

456) Six
457) Maximus
458) Mr. McGregor
459) Harry Truman
460) Red
461) Toto
462) Brazil*

Brazil has won five; Italy and Germany are tied for second with four world cup titles each.

463. Cerro Aconcagua is the highest mountain on which continent?

464. What is the name of the 2001 film in which a shy American girl learns she is the heir to the throne of a European kingdom?

465. What is the name of the highly populated city in the nation of Turkey which is actually located on two continents?

466. What is the most expensive property on the Monopoly game board?

467. In "Star Wars," what is the name of Princess Leia's home planet?

468. Which state is nicknamed "The Golden State"?

469. Although her name was originally Harleen Quinzel, what is the popular DC comics hero better known as?

Answers

463) South America
465) Istanbul*
467) Alderaan
469) Harley Quinn

464) "The Princess Diaries"
466) Boardwalk
468) California

*Istanbul straddles the Bosporus Strait, which divides Europe and Asia. With 15 million residents, it is the most populated city in Europe.

470. Reindeer are known by what other name in North America?

471. What Looney Tunes character often uses the catchphrase "Sufferin' Succotash"?

472. Name the singer whose hits include "Teenage Dream," "Firework," and "Dark Horse."

473. What popular video game takes place mostly on the planet Pandora, and features the characters Claptrap, Handsome Jack, and Marcus Kincaid?

474. What future state was sold to the United States by Russia in 1867?

475. How many pints are in a gallon?

476. What 2001 book, turned into a 2020 movie, tells the story of a 12 year old boy who teams up with a servant, dwarf, and fairy to save his father?

Answers

470) Caribou   471) Sylvester
472) Katy Perry   473) "Borderlands"
474) Alaska*   475) Eight
476) "Artemis Fowl"

*Despite the fact the purchase of Alaska was made for $7 million dollars, roughly two cents an acre, many in Congress and the media criticized it. They called it "Seward's Folly," after Secretary of State William Seward, who made the purchase.

477. What was the name of the famous leader in India who used nonviolent protest to lead his country in breaking away from British rule?

478. Jason Mimoa played the title character in what 2018 D.C. Comics superhero film?

479. In what 2004 film does Tom Hanks provide the adult voice for "Hero Boy?"

480. What letter is not included in the name of any of America's 50 states?

481. What is the title of the second film in the "Pirates of the Caribbean" series?

482. What Nickelodeon series starred Jamie Lynn Spears as a student at a fictional boarding school in Southern California?

483. Which planet is seventh closest to the sun?

Answers

477) Mahatma Gandhi

478) "Aquaman"

479) "Polar Express"

480) Q

481) "Pirates of the Caribbean: Dead Man's Chest"

482) "Zoey 101"*

483) Uranus

*Britney Spears, Jamie Lynn's sister, wrote the original theme song "Follow Me" for Zoey 101, which is sung by Jamie Lynn in the opening credits of the show.

484. What is the native continent of Chinchillas?

485. In the television series "Mickey Mouse Clubhouse," what is the name of the supercomputer that helps Mickey and his friends find answers?

486. The human body contains 206 what?

487. What is the name of the scale that measures the size and severity of an earthquake?

488. What kind of creature is Spongebob Squarepants' best friend Patrick?

489. What is the name of the 2012 children's book by R.J. Palacio about a child named Auggie who has a rare condition which made his face appear disfigured?

490. What mathematical term refers to the answer when two or more numbers are multiplied?

Answers

484) South America*
486) Bones
488) Starfish
490) The product

485) Toodles
487) Richter Scale
489) "Wonder"

*Chinchillas have the thickest fur of any animal which lives on land.

491. The word "dinosaur" comes from the Greek word for "terrible _____."

492. In the television series "Blue's Clues and You!," what is the name of the host, who is a cousin of Steve and Joe, the hosts from the original "Blue's Clues" series.

493. Whose song "God's Plan" spent eleven weeks at No. 1 in 2018 and won the Grammy for Best Rap Song of that year?

494. What is the proper term to call a baby dolphin?

495. What is the name of Bambi's rabbit friend?

496. An improper fraction is always greater than what number?

497. What is the name of the 2012 animated movie based upon a Dr. Seuss book which tells the story of a boy named Ted who lives in a walled city?

Answers

491) Lizard*   492) Josh
493) Drake   494) A calf
495) Thumper   496) One
497) "The Lorax"

*In the Greek language "Deinos" means terrible, and "Sauros" means lizard.

498. In what country would you find the Leaning Tower of Pisa?

499. Whose picture is on the $100 bill?

500. What legendary NFL player has won the most Super Bowls of any individual player?

501. What is the name of the town that the Flintstones lived in?

502. In what country was Justin Bieber born?

503. What marsupial native to Australia eats eucalyptus leaves and attracts a mate by belching?

504. What is the name of the 2020 Disney movie in which a princess dresses up in armor to try to save her father?

Answers

498) Italy
500) Tom Brady*
502) Canada
504) "Mulan"

499) Benjamin Franklin
501) Bedrock
503) Koala

Brady has won seven Super Bowls. The player with the next most is former 49ers and Cowboys linebacker Charles Haley, with five. Brady has appeared in 10 Super Bowls, also a record.

505. Clara Barton is credited with founding what major organization in 1881?

506. What is the name of the 2002 animated film about a boy named Jim Hawkins, on the planet Montressor?

507. What is the name of the popular children's book series which, as of February 2022, has 21 installments with the first subtitled "Miss Daisy is Crazy?"

508. What is the name of Henry Danger's girlfriend?

509. What is the only animal which can move its eyes independently?

510. In what city did Dr. Martin Luther King, Jr., deliver his famous "I Have a Dream" speech?

511. What was happening in the sky on August 21, 2017, that had most Americans looking upward?

Answers

505) The American Red Cross   506) "Treasure Planet"
507) "My Weird School"   508) Piper Hart
509) Chameleon   510) Washington, D.C.
511) Solar Eclipse*

The previous total solar eclipse in the United States was in 1979. Another one will happen in April, 2024.

512. In "The Wild Thornberry," what is the name of the Thornberry's youngest daughter?

513. How many toes does a cat have on each of its back paws?

514. What color is the popular "Tickle Me Elmo" doll?

515. Which country has the most miles of coastline?

516. What popular Christmas song begins with the line, "Sleigh bells ring, are you listening?"

517. In the "Beethoven" film series, what kind of dog is Beethoven?

518. Milk, cheese, and yogurt all fit into what food group?

Answers

512) Eliza
514) Red
516) "Winter Wonderland"
518) Dairy

513) Four*
515) Canada
517) St. Bernard

*Most cats have a total of 18 toes. Five on their front paws and four on the back ones.

519. In the Animal Crossing game series, what kind of animal is Isabella?

520. Which American city is nicknamed "The Big Apple"?

521. Val Kilmer voices the character of Moses in what 1998 animated film?

522. Only two states are completely within the Pacific time zone. One is California. What is the other?

523. What was the last name of the brothers who became the first ever humans to fly an airplane in 1903?

524. What are the tissues that connect muscles to bones known as?

525. How many different colors are the squares in the game "Twister?"

Answers

519) A dog
521) "The Prince of Egypt"
523) Wright
525) Four

520) New York City
522) Washington*
524) Tendons

*Idaho, Nevada, and Oregon include parts that are in the Mountain time zone.

526. In the popular fairy tale "Hansel and Gretel," what did Hansel and Gretel leave on the trail so they could find their way home?

527. What famous bear lives in the forest surrounding the Hundred Acre Wood?

528. Which NFL team features a lightning bolt on its helmet?

529. In order to win a game of "Uno," how many points does a player have to be the first to reach?

530. Which U.S. state only shares a border with one other state?

531. What American is credited with inventing the light bulb and the phonograph?

532. In "Sleeping Beauty," what is the name of the song that Aurora sings in the forest on her 16th birthday?

Answers

526) Breadcrumbs 527) Winnie the Pooh
528) Los Angeles Chargers 529) 500
530) Maine 531) Thomas Edison*
532) "Once Upon a Dream"

*Edison is considered the greatest inventor in American history. He holds more patents than anyone, with 1,093.

533. What planet are the Transformers from?

534. What is the capital city of Mexico?

535. What toy, capable of more than 40 sounds including singing and burping, was the No. 1 selling Christmas toy in America in 2017?

536. Under its white fur, what color is a polar bear's skin?

537. What popular boy band's hits include "Best Song Ever," "Story of My Life," and "What Makes You Beautiful?"

538. What is the name of Iron Man's daughter?

539. What popular children's show features a blue fox named "Fig" and his caterpillar friend named "Stick"?

Answers

533) Cybertron
535) Fingerlings
537) One Direction
539) "Tumble Leaf"

534) Mexico City*
536) Black
538) Morgan Stark

*Mexico City is the most populated city in North America, followed by New York City and Los Angeles.

540. What ocean separates India and Africa?

541. What is the name of Bugs Bunny's girlfriend?

542. What scientist is most famous for proposing three laws of motion?

543. In Pokemon, what color is Pikachu?

544. In the classic nursery rhyme "One, Two, Buckle My Shoe," what four words follow "Three, Four?"

545. In Scrabble, what two letters have the highest point value?

546. What is a shape with eight sides called?

Answers

540) Indian
542) Isaac Newton
544) "Knock on the Door"
546) Octagon

541) Lola
543) Yellow
545) Q and Z*

*Q and Z are each worth ten points, J and X are the next most valuable, each worth eight points.

547. The Thames river runs through what European capital city?

548. What is the first name of the leading dog in the book and movie "A Dog's Way Home"?

549. What popular Nickelodeon series tells the story of a family with superpowers living in the fictional town of "Hiddenville"?

550. What San Diego native nicknamed "Birdman" is considered one of the greatest skateboarders of all time?

551. What is the name of the popular children's book about a boy named Stanley Yelnats, who is sent to a correctional facility in the desert after being falsely accused of stealing?

552. What is the world's fastest two-legged animal?

553. In which state would you find the Hollywood Walk of Fame?

Answers

547) London   548) Bella
549) "The Thundermans"   550) Tony Hawk
551) "Holes"   552) Ostrich*
553) California

The ostrich can run for ten miles at 30 miles per hour!

554. What popular TikTok star and "Cat Rapper" is featured on a Netflix show called "Cat People?"

555. Who is the only president in American history to be elected president more than twice?

556.   What building, located in New York City, was the first in the world to have more than 100 stories?

557. What type of animal is Spongebob's cranky neighbor Squidward Tentacles?

558. Who broke the record for longest No. 1 song of all time in 2021, with a song that is 10 minutes and 13 seconds long?

559. In "Paw Patrol," what is the name of the English Bulldog who knows all about skateboarding and snowboarding?

560. In what part of the human body would you find the smallest bones?

Answers

554) Moshow   555) Franklin D. Roosevelt
556) Empire State Building   557) Octopus
558) Taylor Swift*   559) Rubble
560) The ear

* "All Too Well: Taylor's Version" replaced Don McClean's "American Pie" as the longest song ever to top the charts.

561. What superhero once had a crush on Mary Jane Watson, and will eventually marry her?

562. What is the proper term for an adult female horse?

563. Musical instruments which are played by striking are known as what?

564. In which American city is "The Space Needle" located?

565. What is the most popular color for cars in the United States?

566. As of March, 2022, what singer is married to Jay-Z?

567. The United States, Liberia, and Myanmar are the only three countries in the world that don't use what system of measurement?

Answers

561) Spiderman
563) Percussion
565) White*
567) The metric system

562) A Mare
564) Seattle
566) Beyonce

*White is followed by black, gray, and silver.

568. In the movie "Jurassic Park," Isla Nublar is 40 miles off the coast of what country?

569. Name the popular singer from Barbados whose songs include "What's My Name," "Shut Up and Drive," and "Rude Boy?"

570. On the periodic table of elements, what is the symbol for gold?

571. What is the name of the main villain of the LEGO movie, portrayed by Will Ferrell?

572. What is the name of the fictional town that Arthur, from the popular book and television series, lives in?

573. How many months have 31 days in them?

574. In the popular book "The Very Hungry Caterpillar," what is the first fruit the caterpillar eats?

Answers

568) Costa Rica   569) Rihanna
570) AU   571) "Lord Business" or "President Business"
572) Elwood City   573) Seven*
574) An apple

January, March, May, July, August, October, and December each have 31 days.

575. Which of the United States has the highest yearly rainfall average?

576. In the movie "A Bug's Life," who is the leader of the grasshoppers?

577. What is the name of the children's series in which children detectives, including Agent Otto and Agent Olive, use math skills to solve peculiar problems?

578. By what name was basketball legend Earvin Johnson better known?

579. Which major European city was divided by a wall from 1961 to 1989?

580. In the movie "Maleficent," what is the name of the boy with whom Maleficent falls in love?

581. What is the name of the island that Peter Pan and his friends travel to in order to stay young?

Answers

575) Hawaii*

576) Hopper

577) "Odd Squad"

578) "Magic" Johnson

579) Berlin

580) Stefan

581) Neverland

Hawaii is first in annual rainfall, Louisiana second, Mississippi third, and Alabama fourth.

582. What is the only state with a one syllable name?

583. What is the name of the 2004 animated film in which Will Smith plays a small, underachieving fish named Oscar?

584. In the movie "Toy Story," what is the name of Andy's evil neighbor?

585. What is the second-most populated country in the world?

586. In the book and movie "Matilda," what is the name of Matilda's teacher?

587. Who informed Harry Potter that he was a wizard?

588. In the movie "Brave," what kind of animal does Queen Elinor turn into?

Answers

582) Maine
584) Sid Phillips
586) Miss Honey
588) A bear

583) "Shark Tale"
585) India*
587) Hagrid

*In order, the five most populated countries in the world are: China, India, The United States, Indonesia, and Pakistan.

589. What is the name of the popular cartoon network show about a tiny group of fungi who are guardians of the forest?

590. Who is the youngest Disney princess?

591. In the nursery rhyme "Little Miss Muffet," what was Miss Muffet eating?

592. In what National Park would you find a geyser called "Old Faithful"?

593. Which fast-food chain has the largest number of restaurants in the world?

594. What is "Hello Kitty's" favorite food?

595. What is the first type of animal mentioned in the song "Old MacDonald Had a Farm"?

Answers

589) "Mush-Mush and the Mushables" 590) Snow White*
591) Curds and whey   592) Yellowstone
593) Subway   594) Apple Pie
595) A cow

*Snow White is 14, Jasmine in Aladdin is the next youngest at age 15.

596. How long does it take the Earth to fully orbit the sun?

597. What city is nicknamed "The Windy City?"

598. What is the name of the 2013 movie in which a teenager named Mary Katherine gets teleported to a kingdom filled with talking slugs?

599. In "Guardians of the Galaxy," what type of animal is Rocket?

600. What is the center of a hurricane called?

601. What is the name of the 10-year-old boy who is the main character in the story "The Phantom Tollbooth"?

602. What famous football game, played at the beginning of each year, is nicknamed "The Granddaddy Of Them All?"

Answers

596) One year*   597) Chicago
598) "Epic"   599) A raccoon
600) The eye   601) Milo
602) The Rose Bowl

*To be precise, it takes 365.25 days, causing the need to add an extra day every four years, which is the reasoning behind "leap year."

603. In a famous nursery rhyme, who couldn't be put back together by "all the king's horses and all the king's men?"

604. Which popular breakfast cereal uses "Tony the Tiger" in its advertisements?

605. In the original "Despicable Me" movie, what does felonious Gru plot to steal?

606. What is the name of the highest mountain in the United States?

607. What color are Mickey Mouse's shoes?

608. How many provinces does Canada have?

609. In "True and the Rainbow Kingdom," what is the name of True's best friend, who is a cat?

Answers

603) "Humpty Dumpty"
605) The Moon
607) Yellow
609) Bartleby

604) Frosted Flakes
606) Denali*
608) Ten

*The mountain was named Mt. McKinley until it was officially changed to Denali, the name used by native Alaskans, in 2015 by President Obama.

610. On what planet was Superman born?

611. In "Dora the Explorer," what is the name of the sneaky fox?

612. Cooperstown, New York, is the home to what sport's hall of fame?

613. What is the name of the classic 1982 animated film which features Mrs. Brisby, a widowed field mouse?

614. What is the name of the popular series on the Cartoon Network in which a 10-year-old has the power to turn into ten different aliens?

615. In what state would you find five National Parks, including Zion and Bryce Canyon?

616. What unit of measurement, which is approximately six feet, is used to measure depth of water?

Answers

610) Krypton
612) Baseball
614) "Ben 10"
616) Fathom

611) Swiper
613) "The Secret of NIMH"
615) Utah*

Utah's five national parks are Capitol Reef, Arches, Canyonlands, Bryce Canyon, and Zion.

617. On which popular children's show would you find characters named "Grampy Rabbit," "Daddy Pig," "Pedro Pony," and "Mr. Bull"?

618. What is the name of the fictional world that the popular video game "Super Mario Bros" is set in?

619. What singer had her first No. 1 hit in 2011 with the song "Rolling in the Deep?"

620. How many years are there in a millennium?

621. What is the capital city of China?

622. In "The Little Mermaid II: Return to the Sea," what is the name of the daughter of Ariel and Prince Eric?

623. The "Just Dance" video game series got its name from a song with the same name by what popular artist?

Answers

617) "Peppa Pig"   618) "The Mushroom Kingdom"
619) Adele*   620) 1,000
621) Beijing   622) Melody
623) Lady Gaga

*For a time, the song was the top-selling digital song by a female artist of all time.

624. What is the name of the wooly mammoth in the "Ice Age" film series?

625. In what state would you find Pearl Harbor?

626. What is the name of the popular outdoor toy manufactured by Wham-O which is essentially a long plastic sheet which will have water poured on it by its participants?

627. How many letters are in the alphabet?

628. What continent is home to the Andes Mountains?

629. Which hero intercepted a nuclear missile on its way to New York in the movie "The Avengers?"

630. What is the name of the 2021 animated movie in which the people of Kumandra are divided into five kingdoms: Fang, Heart, Spine, Talon, and Tail?

Answers

624) Manny   625) Hawaii
626) Slip 'N Slide   627) 26
628) South America   629) Iron Man
630) "Raya and the Last Dragon"

The Andes are the longest mountain range in the world, and second only to the Himalayas in average height.

631. What are the only two continents on which you can find wild elephants?

632. What is the name of the fictional island which is the home to "Thomas and Friends?"

633. Incisors, canines, and molars are all types of which body part?

634. What is the name of the 2011 film about Bethany Hamilton, who lost her arm as the result of a shark attack while surfing?

635. Taylor Swift is the spokesperson for the NHL team known as the Predators. What city do they represent?

636. What is the name of the Dolphin whose rescue was made into the movie "Dolphin Tale?"

637. What is the name of the television series about a boy named Finn and his best friend Jake who live in the Land of Ooo?

Answers

631) Africa and Asia
633) Teeth
635) Nashville*
637) "Adventure Time"

632) Sodor
634) "Soul Surfer"
636) Winter

Swift was born in Pennsylvania but moved near Nashville when she was 13 to pursue her musical career.

638. In the movie "Encanto," in what country is the village from which Alma is forced to flee?

639. What is the name of the female mouse who is also a pilot and mechanic in the series "Chip and Dale: Rescue Rangers"?

640. What state has the most national parks?

641. What famous singer wrote the majority of the songs for the original "Lion King" movie?

642. What is the name of the famous baseball stadium in Boston, whose left field wall is known as "The Green Monster"?

643. Led by Megatron, what are the main enemies of "The Transformers" called?

644. How many stripes are there on the United States flag?

Answers

638) Colombia
640) California*
642) Fenway Park
644) 13

639) Gadget
641) Elton John
643) The Decepticons

California has nine national parks: The Redwoods, Yosemite, Death Valley, Sequoia, Kings Canyon, Mt. Lassen, Joshua Tree, Pinnacles, and Channel Island.

645. Which country eats the most fish each year?

646. What is the name of the popular book, movie, and television series about a group of friends who run a service taking care of kids in Stoneybrook, Connecticut?

647. The New Zealand All Blacks are a team which begins each contest with a dance known as the Haka to display the team's pride, strength, and unity. In what sport do they compete?

648. What is the only U.S. state to share a border with Canada's Yukon Territories?

649. How many brothers and sisters does Barbie have?

650. What is the tallest animal in the world?

651. Shan Yu is the villain and leader of the Hun Army in what Disney movie?

Answers

645) China
647) Rugby
649) Seven*
651) "Mulan"

646) "The Baby-Sitters Club"
648) Alaska
650) Giraffe

Barbie's seven siblings are: Skipper, Todd, Tutti, Stacie, Chelsea, Kelly, and Krissy.

652.   Egon, Peter, Ray, and Winston are the first names of the original four what?

653.   What is the longest mountain range in the United States?

654.   What is the name of the baking show on YouTube hosted by Rosanna Pansino?

655.   In the movie "Madagascar," what is the name of the hippo?

656.   What famous race is held each May at Churchill Downs?

657.   Who was the youngest person ever to be a president of the United States?

658.   In the movie "Cars," what color is Doc Hudson's car?

Answers

652) Ghostbusters

653) The Rockies

654) "Nerdy Nummies"

655) Gloria

656) The Kentucky Derby

657) Theodore Roosevelt*

658) Blue

*Theodore Roosevelt became president at the age of 42 following the assassination of William McKinley. John F. Kennedy was the youngest person elected president, at the age of 43 in 1960.

659. What color is the substance known as chlorophyll?

660. "Fairy Floss" was invented by a dentist in 1897. By what name is it now more commonly known?

661. What is the largest American lake west of the Mississippi River?

662. What is the name of the princess in "The Princess and the Frog?"

663. The most powerful earthquake in the history of North America occurred in 1964. In what state did it happen?

664. What is the name of the first book of the Bible?

665. "Chip Skylark" is a popular singing sensation on what cartoon show?

Answers

659) Green
661) The Great Salt Lake
663) Alaska*
665) "Fairly OddParents"

660) "Cotton Candy"
662) Tiana
664) Genesis

*The earthquake measured 9.2 on the Richter Scale and resulted in 131 deaths.

666. What 2018 film was the first ever comic superhero movie to be nominated for the Academy Award for Best Picture?

667. What type of animal is Curious George?

668. In decimal form, what is the proper way to express four fifths?

669. What is the only state to be spelled with four S's?

670. Paul McCartney, George Harrison, Ringo Starr, and John Lennon were once a part of what famous band?

671. Abel Tesfaye, who performed at halftime of the Super Bowl in 2021, is better known by what name?

672. From what kind of animal does the fabric known as wool come?

Answers

666) "Black Panther"*   667) Monkey
668) 0.8   669) Mississippi
670) The Beatles   671) The Weeknd
672) Sheep

*"Black Panther" did win three Academy Awards, but lost the Best Picture award to "Green Book."

673. What is the TikTok handle of former hairdresser and star who gained more than 40 million followers by creating a number of characters including her most famous one, Janet.

674. In what country was the fashion company "H. and M." founded in?

675. The Goliath birdeater is the largest of what type of creature?

676. What is the name of the famous ship which sank while it was attempting to travel from England to the United States in 1912?

677. In the popular Netflix series "Sharkdog," what is the name of Sharkdog's 10-year-old best friend?

678. The author of the series of young adult books titled "The Land of Stories" once starred as Kurt Hummel on what popular television series?

679. In which American city would you find the Golden Gate Bridge?

Answers

673) Kallmekris   674) Sweden
675) Spider*   676) Titanic
677) Max   678) "Glee"
679) San Francisco

*The Goliath Birdeater is the largest spider by mass, and is found in northern South America.

680. In what city is the 2018 film "Mary Poppins Returns" set?

681. In which country would you find the Taj Mahal?

682. The penny-farthing was the first machine associated with which popular form of transportation?

683. In what popular video game do players try to save Metro City from President Stone and his robot army?

684. In the animated movie "Song of the Sea," what is the name of Ben's sister?

685. In the game of basketball, typically how high is the rim?

686. In the book and movie "The One and Only Ivan," what type of animal is Ivan?

Answers

680) London
682) Bicycle
684) Saoirse
686) Gorilla

681) India*
683) "Astro Boy"
685) Ten feet

*The Taj Mahal was built in the 160's by Emperor Shah Jahan as a tomb and tribute to his favorite wife.

687.   What is the slowest fish in the ocean?

688.   Which American state has the fewest people?

689.   What insect causes more human death than any other creature each year?

690.   What is the name of Billie Eilish's brother?

691.   A pandemonium is a group of which type of birds?

692.   In "The Three Little Pigs," what did the first pig use to build his house?

693.   The original of what popular movie series featured characters Eric Lehnsherr, Scott Summers, and Ororo Munroe?

Answers

687) The Seahorse

688) Wyoming

689) Mosquito*

690) Finneas

691) Parrots

692) Straw

693) "X-Men"

*It is estimated that mosquitos kill nearly one million people per year.

694. What is Harry Potter's middle name?

695. In square miles, what is the largest country in South America?

696. "Just Do It" is the motto of what shoe and clothing company?

697. The Howler Monkey holds the honor of being the _____ land animal in the world.

698. What famous writer and actor wrote songs for the Disney movie "Encanto"?

699. What is the only U.S. state which ends in the letter "H"?

700. Cinderella's slipper was made of what material?

Answers

694) James
696) Nike
698) Lin-Manuel Miranda
700) Glass

695) Brazil
697) Loudest*
699) Utah

*Overall, the blue whale is the loudest animal in the world.

701. By square miles, what is the third largest state in America?

702. What famous American song was written by Francis Scott Key after he saw the American still flying after a battle in the war of 1812 at Ft. McHenry?

703. In the video game "Minecraft," what is the creeper called after it is struck by lightning?

704. What is the name of the doctor from books and movies who can talk to animals and has a parrot named Polynesia?

705. In "The Wizard of Oz," which character is hoping to get a brain?

706. Lara Croft is the star of what video game series?

707. How many wheels does a semi-trailer truck normally have?

Answers

701) California
703) A Charged Creeper
705) The Scarecrow
707) Eighteen

702) The Star Spangled Banner*
704) Dr. Dolittle
706) "Tomb Raider"

*Originally, the song was written by Key as a poem titled "The Defense of Fort M'Henry."

708. Theodore Roosevelt was the first American president to win which highly regarded prize?

709. In "Rugrats," who is Tommy's best friend?

710. How many planets in the Solar System are smaller than Earth?

711. On what day of the year does the convenience store 711 give away free slurpees?

712. What is the name of the largest rainforest in the world?

713. Which American city is often referred to as "The Big D?"

714. On what date is "Saint Patrick's Day" celebrated each year?

Answers

708) Nobel Peace Prize
709) Chuckie
710) Three*
711) July 11
712) Amazon Rainforest
713) Dallas
714) March 17

*Mercury, Mars, and Venus are each smaller than Earth. (Remember....Pluto is no longer classified as a planet.)

715. What is the capital city of Canada?

716. In "The Incredibles," what is the name of the boy who Violet has a crush on?

717. Name the author who wrote "The Hobbit" and the "Lord of the Rings" series.

718. In the nursery rhyme "Little Jack Horner," what type of pie was Jack eating?

719. What character is the official mascot of Universal Studios?

720. In the French language, what word means "hello"?

721. What is the favorite food of "The Teenage Mutant Ninja Turtles?"

Answers

715) Ottawa
717) J.R.R. Tolkien*
719) Woody Woodpecker
721) Pizza

716) Tony
718) Christmas pie
720) Bonjour

*"Lord of the Rings" has sold more than 150 million copies, making it one of the best-selling books in world history.

722. Pacha, Yzma, Kronk and Chica are all characters in what 2000 Disney movie?

723. In "Lady and the Tramp," what type of dog is Lady?

724. What is the most southern state in the United States?

725. Which fast food restaurant uses the slogan "Think Outside the Bun"?

726. What type of dinosaur is the mascot for Toronto's NBA basketball team?

727. What is the name of the Disney Channel series about a pair of twin brothers who live at the Tipton Hotel?

728. What is the name of Bob the Builder's cat?

Answers

722) "The Emperor's New Groove"   723) Cocker Spaniel
724) Hawaii*   725) Taco Bell
726) Raptor   727) "The Suite Life of
728) Pilchard   Zack and Cody"

*Florida is the southernmost state amongst what are considered the "continental" states.

729. In what state did the Wright brothers become the first humans to fly an airplane in 1903?

730. Mount Kilimanjaro is the highest mountain on which continent?

731. In "Home Alone 2," to what state does Kevin's family travel for Christmas?

732. Mike Wazowski, Randall Boggs, and James Sullivan are characters from which Disney movie?

733. How many strings does a bass guitar normally have?

734. What does the "B" stand for in "SCUBA?"

735. In "SpongeBob SquarePants," what is the name of SpongeBob's pet snail?

Answers

729) North Carolina   730) Africa
731) Florida   732) "Monsters, Inc."
733) Four   734) Breathing*
735) Gary

* "SCUBA" stands for Self-Contained Underwater Breathing Apparatus.

736. What is the name of the instrument used to measure angles in geometry?

737. In "Aladdin," what is the name of Jasmine's pet tiger?

738. In the sport of tennis, what word is used instead of saying "zero" when referring to the score of the game?

739. In the movie "Babe," what kind of animal is Babe?

740. Which clothing brand uses the slogan "Quality never goes out of style"?

741. What is the top selling flavor of Girl Scout cookies?

742. What is the name of the Transformer that is a small yellow Volkswagen Beetle?

Answers

736) Protractor
738) Love
740) Levi Strauss
742) Bumblebee

737) Rajah
739) A pig
741) Thin Mint*

* According to Girl Scouts of America, Thin Mints are followed by Caramel deLites/Samoas, Peanut Butter Patties/Tagalongs, and Do-Si-Dos/Peanut Butter Sandwiches.

743. In which state would you find Mt. Rushmore?

744. What is the name of the village where Franklin the Turtle lives?

745. According to the popular nursery rhyme and children's song, how many monkeys were jumping on the bed?

746. What is the name of popular YouTube star Evan Breeze's sister?

747. In baseball and softball, what do the letters "DH" stand for?

748. In which sea is the nation of Cuba located?

749. What is the name of the former thief who falls in love with Rapunzel in the movie "Tangled?"

Answers

743) South Dakota*
745) Five
747) Designated Hitter
749) Flynn Rider

744) Woodland
746) Jillian
748) Caribbean

* The presidents on Mt. Rushmore are Theodore Roosevelt, George Washington, Thomas Jefferson, and Abraham Lincoln.

750. What country's flag is known as the "Union Jack"?

751. In "Angry Birds," what color is the bird named Chuck?

752. What is the only continent on which no bees live?

753. How many centimeters are there in a meter?

754. In what movie do orphans sing a song titled "Food, Glorious Food?"

755. In a deck of cards, which of the four kings does not have a mustache?

756. What female artist won the Grammy for Album of the Year in 2019 with her album "Golden Hour," which included the songs "Rainbow," "High Horse," and "Slow Burn"?

Answers

750) United Kingdom
752) Antarctica
754) "Oliver!"
756) Kacey Musgraves

751) Yellow
753) 100
755) The King of Hearts*

The King of Hearts is also the only king with a sword through its head.

757. In the comic strip "Peanuts", what is the name of Snoopy's yellow pet bird?

758. In what state would you find Crater Lake National Park?

759. What is the only continent on which emus are native?

760. In what month do Americans celebrate Labor Day?

761. In "The Sound of Music," how many Von Trapp children are there?

762. In the history of the modern Olympic games, which country has won the most medals?

763. What letter do the names of all three of Shrek's children begin with?

Answers

757) Woodstock
759) Australia
761) Seven
763) F

758) Oregon
760) September
762) The United States*

*The Soviet Union/Russia is second, followed by Germany, Great Britain, and France.

764. Freddie Mercury was once the lead singer of what band, which is a member of the Rock and Roll Hall of Fame?

765. Which Mexican food comes from the Spanish word for "Little Donkey"?

766. Who was the second president of the United States?

767. In the animated series "Steven Universe," what is the name of the fictional town in which Steven lives?

768. What Roman numeral symbol represents 10?

769. Which state is nicknamed "The Peach State"?

770. Pink Lady, McIntosh, Granny Smith, and Red Delicious are all types of what fruit?

Answers

764) Queen
766) John Adams
768) X
770) Apple*

765) Burrito
767) Beach City
769) Georgia

The nation of China consumes the most apples each year, followed by the United States and Turkey

771. How many sides does a heptagon have?

772. What artist had a hit in 2015 with her song "Cool For the Summer"?

773. What is the name of Rudolph the Red-Nosed Reindeer's father?

774. Of a dog's five senses, which is the most developed?

775. What was the title of the 2016 sequel to "Finding Nemo"?

776. When it comes to computers, what does "C.P.U." stand for?

777. What is the name of the character who Miley Cyrus voiced in the movie "Bolt"?

Answers

771) Seven
773) Donner
775) "Finding Dory"
777) Penny

772) Demi Lovato
774) Smell*
776) Central Processing Unit

*The portion of the dog's brain that is devoted to analyzing smell is about 40 times more than that of a human.

778. In a deck of cards, how many Jacks have only one eye?

779. In the movie "Inside Out," what is the name of the 11-year-old girl who moves from Minnesota to San Francisco?

780. What is it called when a golfer completes a hole in two shots less than par?

781. In "Pop Goes the Weasel," around what kind of bench did the monkey chase the weasel?

782. Bangkok is the capital city of what country?

783. What is the name of Taylor Swift's album which is also the year she was born?

784. An archipelago is a group of _____.

Answers

778) Two*

779) Riley

780) An eagle

781) Cobbler's Bench

782) Thailand

783) 1989

784) Islands

The Jack of Spades and the Jack of Hearts.

785. What major university's sports teams are known as "The Longhorns"?

786. What is the name of the medic for the "Octonauts"?

787. How many different colors are there on a Rubik's Cube?

788. In "Toy Story," what kind of animal is "Bullseye"?

789. Who won the Nobel Prize for physics in 1921 for his explanation of the photoelectric effect?

790. What is the name of the river that forms a 1255 mile portion of the border between the United States and Mexico?

791. In the animated movie "The Mitchells Vs. Machines," what is the name of the aspiring filmmaker and the daughter of Rick?

Answers

785) The University of Texas
786) Peso Penguin
787) Six*
788) Horse
789) Albert Einstein
790) The Rio Grande
791) Katie

* The colors are white, red, orange, blue, green, and yellow.

792. What is the name of the game in which a speaker tries to trick a group by saying (or not saying) a certain phrase to tell them what to do?

793. In the original movie "Cars," who wins the Piston Cup?

794. As of 2022, who is the oldest president in the history of the United States?

795. What famous scientist was born the exact same day as Abraham Lincoln: February 12, 1809?

796. What mega-star had his first major role starring in the television series "The Fresh Prince of Bel-Air"?

797. What is the name of Yogi Bear's best friend?

798. In what country does "The Little Mermaid" take place?

Answers

792) Simon Says
794) Joe Biden*
796) Will Smith
798) Denmark

793) Chick Hicks
795) Charles Darwin
797) Boo-Boo

*The second-oldest President in American history was Donald Trump, followed by Ronald Reagan.

799. What is the name of the popular video game in which players slice fruit with a blade controlled by touch screen?

800. In the Nickelodeon series "Big Time Rush," the four band members used to play what sport?

801. The cornea, pupil, and iris can all be found in which part of the human body?

802. What state is known as "The Keystone State"?

803. By what name is Instagram star Lilliana Ketchman better known?

804. How many years did Sleeping Beauty sleep?

805. Whose picture is on the $1 bill?

Answers

799) "Fruit Ninja"   800) Hockey
801) The eye   802) Pennsylvania*
803) Lilly K   804) 100 years
805) George Washington

*A keystone is a wedge shaped piece that keeps the other pieces in an arch together. Hence, because of Pennsylvania's central location in the original 13 states, it was seen as essential in keeping the union together.

806. What is the name of the classic children's book written by Shel Silverstein which follows the relationship between a boy and an apple tree?

807. What is the most visited theme park in the world?

808. "Happier Than Ever" is the title to the second studio album released by what star on July 30, 2021?

809. What color belt is worn by beginners at karate?

810. On the Disney Channel series "Amphibia," what is the name of the family of frogs who take Anne in?

811. In the movie "Madagascar," what kind of animal is Marty?

812. Which bird is considered the universal symbol for peace?

Answers

806) "The Giving Tree"   807) Disneyworld*
808) Billie Eilish   809) White
810) The Plantars   811) Zebra
812) The Dove

*In 2019, the second-most visited is Disneyland in California, the third was Disneyland Tokyo.

813. What is the capital city of Spain?

814. How many legs does a mosquito have?

815. Roger Moore, Sean Connery, Daniel Craig, and Pierce Brosnan have all played what famous movie role?

816. What is the name of 1994 movie about a young football team which includes a player named Becky "Icebox" O'Shea?

817. What city is nicknamed "The City of Angels"

818. In the film "The Secret Life of Pets," what is Max's owner's name?

819. Which Pokemon has the ability to control time?

Answers

813) Madrid
815) James Bond
817) Los Angeles*
819) Dialga

814) Six
816) "Little Giants"
818) Katie

* The original full name of Los Angeles was Nuestra Senora La Reina de Los Angeles de Prociuncula.

820. Name the 2015 Disney Channel original movie about 16-year-old Monica Reeves, who is determined to overcome challenges to become Prom Queen.

821. In the United States, what month is observed as "Black History Month?"

822. After how many personal fouls is a player ejected from an NBA game?

823. What is the name of the river that flows through the Grand Canyon?

824. In the movie "Ant-Man," where does Scott Lang get a job when he is released from prison?

825. What is another term more commonly used for "Aurora Borealis?"

826. What is the name of the musical film in which Mickey Mouse appears as a magician?

Answers

820) "Bad Hair Day"   821) February
822) Six   823) The Colorado
824) Baskin-Robbins   825) Northern Lights*
826) "Fantasia"

*When the same lighting effect happens in the southern hemisphere, it is known as "Aurora Australis."

827. In the movie "Frozen," what is the name of Anna and Elsa's kingdom?

828. In 2002, Kelly Clarkson became the first contestant to win what popular television series?

829. What is the name of the medieval British king famous for having a round table?

830. In the popular video game series, what is the name of Mario's twin brother?

831. Which country is also referred to as "The Netherlands?"

832. In "Courage the Cowardly Dog," where were Courage's parents sent by an evil veterinarian?

833. The song "When You Wish Upon a Star" first appeared in what classic animated movie?

Answers

827) Arendelle
828) "American Idol"
829) King Arthur*
830) Luigi
831) Holland
832) Outer Space
833) Pinocchio

*Historians argue on how true many of the stories of King Arthur are, but he allegedly had a round table so that none of his barons would feel superior or inferior to any of the others.

834. Who in 1932 became the first woman to fly solo across the Atlantic Ocean?

835. In "Boss Baby" what is the name of the liquid which makes babies and old people smell more lovely?

836. The pectoralis major and pectoralis minor are muscles found in which part of the human body?

837. On what month and day each year is "Groundhog Day" in America?

838. Inside of what sea creature are pearls found?

839. In the movie "Up," to what continent do Carl and Russell travel?

840. What color is Octopus blood?

Answers

834) Amelia Earhart
835) Stinkless Serum
836) The chest
837) February 2
838) Oysters
839) South America
840) Blue*

Snails and spiders also have blue blood.

841. In the movie "Bambi," what kind of animal is the character named "Flower?"

842. What is the only uniform number that Tom Brady wore in his NFL career?

843. How many years are United States senators elected for?

844. In "The Lego Movie," what is Emmet's last name?

845. What month and day do many fans celebrate "Star Wars Day?"

846. In the movie "Ice Age," what kind of animal is Sid?

847. In what country would you find the Ganges River?

Answers

841) Skunk
843) Six years
845) May 4846) A sloth
847) India

842) 12*
844) Brickowski

*Although he wore number 12 for both the Patriots and Buccaneers, Brady wore the number 10 while playing his college football at the University of Michigan.

848. When it comes to computers, what does "www" stand for?

849. In "Little Red Riding Hood," who does the wolf dress up as?

850. On what Mexican holiday is the movie "Coco" based?

851. Who is the Swedish environmental activist who in 2019 became the youngest person ever to be named Time Magazine's "Person of the Year"?

852. What is the proper term for what are often referred to as "shooting stars"?

853. In what sport do athletes compete for the Vince Lombardi trophy?

854. Which European country shares its border with the most countries?

Answers

848) World Wide Web   849) Grandmother
850) The Day of the Dead   851) Greta Thunberg
852) Meteorites   853) Football
854) Germany*

Germany is bordered by nine countries: Denmark, Austria, Switzerland, the Czech Republic, Poland, France, Belgium, Luxembourg, and the Netherlands.

855. In the song "America the Beautiful," what color are the waves of grain?

856. In "Scooby Doo," what is Shaggy's last name?

857. In "Clifford the Big Red Dog," what color is the bulldog named "T-Bone"?

858. What is the name of the official currency used in Mexico?

859. From what country did the United States buy the Louisiana Purchase?

860. In which state would you find a town called "Tombstone," the site of the historic "gunfight at the O.K. Corral"?

861. What popular candy uses the slogan, "Melts in your mouth, not in your hands"?

Answers

855) Amber
857) Yellow
859) France
861) M&M's*

856) Rogers
858) Peso
860) Arizona

*According to Mentalfloss.com, M&M's are the most popular chocolate treat in America.

862. What is the proper name for animals which develop their babies in the mother's pouch?

863. What country's flag features an eagle holding a snake in its mouth?

864. In the 2021 animated movie "Rumble," in what sport do monsters compete?

865. What are the tubes in the human body which carry blood back to the heart called?

866. What type of insect is WALL-E's friend Hal in the movie "Wall-E?"

867. How many toes do sheep have on each foot?

868. In "The Lion King," what is the name of Simba's Uncle?

Answers

862) Marsupials
864) Wrestling
866) Cockroach
868) Scar

863) Mexico
865) Veins*
867) Two

* Arteries carry blood and nutrients away from the heart, while veins return them to the heart.

869. A group of what type of birds is known as a "murder"?

870. What is the name of the 2000 movie about a group of chickens that live on an egg farm run by the evil Mrs. Tweedy and her husband?

871. Which farm animal is incapable of looking directly up?

872. Which female superstar performed her hits "Poker Face" and "Born This Way" during the halftime show of Super Bowl 51?

873. How many days are in a "fortnight"?

874. What is the capital city of Colorado?

875. One of the most popular Christmas songs of all time is "All I Want For Christmas is You," by what artist?

Answers

869) Crows
871) Pigs
873) 14874) Denver
875) Mariah Carey*

870) "Chicken Run"
872) Lady Gaga

* "All I Want for Christmas is You" is the best-selling holiday song by a female artist of all time.

876. In "The Fantastic Mr. Fox," what is Mr. Fox's son's name?

877. The formula "½ multiplied by base, multiplied by height" will give you the area of what shape?

878. What is Big Bird's teddy bear named?

879. What is the name of the weather instrument used to measure atmospheric pressure?

880. When doing "The Hokey Pokey," what is the first body part you are supposed to put in?

881. In "Peanuts," how much does Lucy charge for Psychiatric help?

882. In the movie "Annie," what is Annie's dog's name?

Answers

876) Ash
878) Radar
880) Right Foot
882) Sandy

877) A triangle
879) Barometer*
881) Five cents.

*Barometric pressure is a key component in predicting future weather.

883.   In what country did Yoga originate?

884.   In the book "The Treasure Island," what is the name of Long John Silver's parrot?

885.   Which of Harry Potter's friends became a herbology teacher at Hogwarts?

886.   In the movie "Brave," on which birthday is Princess Merida given a bow and arrow by her father?

887.   In "Mr. Rogers' Neighborhood," what is Mr. Rogers' first name?

888.   Words that sound the same but have different meanings are known as what?

889.   What is the most populous city in the state of Texas?

Answers

883) India

884) Captain Flint

885) Pomona Sprout

886) 6th birthday

887) Fred

888) Homonyms

889) Houston*

Houston is followed by Dallas, San Antonio, and Austin.

890. In the popular children's nursery rhyme "Pat-A-Cake, Pat-A-Cake," what letter is the baker's man supposed to mark the cake with?

891. In the movie "Minions," the Minions are driven into isolation because they fired a cannon at what famous historical leader?

892. What popular Nickelodeon series told the story of Tori Vega, who attends a high school called "The Hollywood School for the Arts?"

893. Sedimentary, metamorphic, and igneous are all types of what?

894. What is the name of the animated television series about an 8-year-old pirate named Santiago Montes?

895. Which reptile is known for its ability to change its body color?

896. What is the name of the 2008 film based on the music of the pop group "ABBA"?

Answers

890) B

892) "Victorious"

894) "Santiago of the Seas"

896) "Mamma Mia"

891) Napoleon

893) Rocks

895) Chameleon*

*A chameleon can change its color in about 20 seconds. Half of all species of chameleons live on the island of Madagascar.

897. What is a hole in a tooth known as?

898. In the Dr. Seuss book "Cat in the Hat," what two colors are the cat's top hat?

899. What is Superman's human name?

900. In "The Wizard of Oz," from what state is Dorothy?

901. Which country consumes the most chocolate per person each year?

902. How many sides does a stop sign normally have?

903. Who wrote "James and the Giant Peach" and "Matilda"?

Answers

897) Cavity

899) Clark Kent

901) Switzerland*

903) Roald Dahl

898) Red and white

900) Kansas

902) Eight

Switzerland is followed by Austria, Germany, Ireland, and Great Britain.

904. Whose face is pictured on the dime?

905. What state is nicknamed "The Aloha State"?

906. In Monsters, Inc., how many eyes does Mr. Waternoose have?

907. The Mariana Trench is the deepest part of any ocean in the world. In which ocean would you find it?

908. In what year did the COVID-19 pandemic begin?

909. In the classic movie "Cinderella," what creatures wake Cinderella up at the start of the film?

910. What does the acronym YOLO stand for?

Answers

904) Franklin D. Roosevelt   905) Hawaii
906) Five   907) The Pacific
908) 2019*   909) Birds
910) You Only Live Once

* COVID-19 represents Coronavirus Disease 2019.

911. What is the name of the cheetah who serves as the mascot for Cheetos?

912. What is the name of the mountain range that stretches from California to Canada, and through Oregon and Washington?

913. What are the first names of the two fourth grade boys who created Captain Underpants?

914. In "Sesame Street," who is Ernie's best friend?

915. What is the name of the famous female leader of the Underground Railroad who is set to have her picture on the $20 bill by the year 2030?

916. Which state uses the motto "The Equality State," because it was the first to grant women the right to vote?

917. In "Frozen," what is the name of the snowman?

Answers

911) Chester
913) George and Harold
915) Harriet Tubman
917) Olaf

912) The Cascades
914) Bert
916) Wyoming*

*Women in Wyoming got the right to vote in 1869. It did not become a right for all women in America though until 1920.

918. Which city in the American west is nicknamed "The Emerald City"?

919. In what month do Americans celebrate "Presidents Day"?

920. Although most of Barney is purple, what color is his tummy?

921. What is the name of the Disney Channel series which focuses on the Duncan family of Denver and their new challenges of having five children?

922. What is the name of the snowboarder who competed for the American Olympic team in five Olympics, winning three gold medals, who announced his retirement in 2022?

923. What state features the most peaks taller than 14,000 feet?

924. What activity are you doing if you are doing positions known as "cat," "cobra," or "downward-facing dog"?

Answers

918) Seattle
920) Green
922) Shaun White
924) Yoga

919) February*
921) "Good Luck Charlie"
923) Colorado

*President's Day is on the third Monday of each February. February was chosen because it includes the birthdays of both George Washington and Abraham Lincoln.

925. What is the name of the decimal system that is used to help locate and organize books in a library?

926. What can be counted on a tree to determine how old it is?

927. In the movie "Willy Wonka and the Chocolate Factory," what are the small people called?

928. What is the name of the ghost who is criticized by his three wicked uncles, who are known as "The Ghastly Trio?"

929. In "Avatar: The Last Airbender," there are four nations: earth, water, fire, and what?

930. In the Spanish language, what is the proper way to say the number one?

931. "An Innocent Warrior," "Know Who You Are," and "How Far I'll Go," are on songs featured on the soundtrack of what 2016 film?

Answers

925) The Dewey Decimal System   926) The rings
927) Oompa- Loompas   928) Casper
929) Air   930) Uno
931) "Moana"*

*The "Moana" soundtrack was the fifth-best selling album of 2016.

932. On which side of the human body is the heart normally found?

933. What is Miley Cyrus's real first name?

934. Who was the first Disney Princess to have a child?

935. Who released the album "Oops I Did it Again" in the year 2000?

936. What are the names of "Iron Man" Tony Stark's parents?

937. Who is the Italian artist who painted the ceiling of the Sistine Chapel?

938. The leprechaun is associated with which day of celebration each March?

Answers

932) Left
934) Ariel
936) Howard and Maria
938) St. Patrick's Day

933) Destiny*
935) Britney Spears
937) Michelangelo

*Her father, country music star Billy Ray Cyrus, and mother named her "Destiny Hope" because they believed she would accomplish great things.

939. What fashion brand is known for its polo shirts?

940. In the movie "The Trolls," what are the names of the creatures who are trying to eat the Trolls?

941. What band released their debut album titled "2 Cool 4 Skool" in 2013?

942. In the Periodic Table, which element is represented by "Fe"?

943. On the classic children's show "Rocky and Bullwinkle," what kind of animal is Bullwinkle?

944. In which board game can you find characters named Colonel Mustard, Professor Plum, and Mrs. Peacock?

945. What is the name of the national park where Yogi Bear lives?

Answers

939) Ralph Lauren

940) The Bergens

941) BTS*

942) Iron

943) Moose

944) "Clue"

945) Jellystone National Park

*BTS is the fastest group to have five No. 1 singles since Michael Jackson.

946. In the movie "Madagascar," from what zoo do the animals escape?

947. Santiago is the capital city of what South American country?

948. "Solid Snake" is a hero in which video game series?

949. The artist "Tones and I" had an international smash hit in 2019 with what song?

950. How many Olympic rings are there?

951. What do Americans celebrate each February 14?

952. In "101 Dalmatians," what is the first name of the lady that Roger Radcliffe marries?

Answers

946) Central Park Zoo
948) Metal Gear
950) Five
952) Anita

947) Chile
949) "Dance Monkey"*
951) Valentine's Day

* "Monkey Dance" broke the record for song with most weeks at No. 1 in the U.K. by a female artist.

953. What is the only country in the world whose name ends with the letter "Q"?

954. What does the acronym "DIY" stand for?

955. In "Thumbelina," what kind of a creature carries Thumbelina off in the hope that she will marry her son?

956. In "Aquaman," what is the name of Aquaman's sidekick?

957. The names of the two imaginary lines which circle the earth parallel to the equator are the Tropic of Cancer and the Tropic of _____.

958. What is the first letter in the Greek alphabet?

959. In what sport do athletes compete for the Ryder Cup?

Answers

953) Iraq
955) A toad
957) Capricorn
959) Golf*

954) Do it yourself
956) Aqualad
958) Alpha

*The Ryder Cup pits a team of the top players from the United States vs. the top players in Europe.

960. In the movie "Up," what job did Carl Fredrickson do before retiring?

961. Cairo is the capital city of what country?

962. In "Space Jam," what is the name of the Looney Toons team?

963. What color cap does Papa Smurf almost always wear?

964. What are the three primary colors?

965. In a game of pool, what color is the ball with the number 2 on it?

966. What kind of creature is Stuart Little?

Answers

960) Sold balloons

961) Egypt

962) Tune Squad

963) Red

964) Red, green, and blue

965) Blue*

966) A mouse

*Balls one through eight are all solid colors. Nine through fifteen have a stripe.

967. In "Duck Tales," what is the name of Huey, Dewey, and Louie's mother?

968. Which television network hosts "The Teen Choice Awards" each year?

969. What type of dog is Scooby Doo?

970. In the board game "Monopoly," how much money is a player rewarded when they pass go?

971. Name the singer who had her first No. 1 hit with her 2019 song "Lose You to Love Me."

972. The English Channel connects England with what country?

973. "Jumbeaux's Café" is an ice cream parlor set up mainly for elephants and large animals in what movie?

Answers

967) Della
969) Great Dane
971) Selena Gomez
973) "Zootopia"

968) FOX*
970) $200
972) France

*Nickelodeon hosts a similar event, geared towards a slightly younger audience known as "The Kid's Choice Awards"

974. What was the primary occupation of Florence Nightingale?

975. Where would you find "The Sea of Tranquility"?

976. In "Tangled," what are the names of Rapunzel's parents?

977. In "Paw Patrol," what type of dog is Marshall?

978. In Major League Baseball, players at what position compete for the Cy Young Award?

979. What is the most common eye color in humans?

980. What movie series includes a main character named Carmen Cortez?

Answers

974) A nurse
976) Queen Arianna and King Frederic
978) Pitchers*
980) "Spy Kids"

975) The Moon
977) Dalmatian
979) Brown

*The award is named for Cy Young, who won 511 games, more than any other pitcher in history. He also holds the records with most losses, with 315.

981. Who was the president of the United States immediately before Donald Trump?

982. In "Transformers," who is the leader of the Dinobots?

983. Each Fourth of July, Nathan's hosts a contest in New York City to see who can eat the most what?

984. In "Iron Man 3," what is the name of the villain played by Ben Kingsely?

985. Sudden movements along fault lines within Earth cause what potentially dangerous natural phenomenon to occur?

986. In "The Loud House," what is the name of Lincoln's oldest sister?

987. Harvard, Tufts, and Amherst are all highly regarded universities in which state?

Answers

981) Barack Obama   982) Grimlock
983) Hot Dogs*   984) Trevor Slattery (Mandarin)
985) Earthquakes   986) Lori
987) Massachusetts

Contestants are given ten minutes to eat as many hot dogs as they can, including buns. In 2021, Joey Chestnut set the world record by eating 76.

988. In "A Charlie Brown Christmas," Sally writes a letter to Santa Claus asking for a gift. What is the gift she wants?

989. Americans honor those who have served on Veteran's Day each year. What day of the year does it fall?

990. What is the name of the uncle in "The Addams Family"?

991. In Disney's "Bear in the Big Blue House," what kind of creatures are Pip and Pop?

992. "Bubblegum Troll" is a major enemy of players in what popular video game?

993. What famous company was founded in 1976 by Steve Jobs and Steve Wozniak?

994. What is the name of the dog in "Tom and Jerry?"

Answers

988) Money

989) November 11*

990) Fester

991) Otters

992) Candy Crush Saga

993) Apple

994) Spike

*November 11, 1918, is the day that World War One ended. "Armistice Day" was observed on that day until it was changed to "Veterans Day" in 1954.

995. At 590 miles wide, Ceres is the largest _____ in our Solar System.

996. What is the name of the volcano that erupted in the state of Washington in May of 1980?

997. What is the name of the blueish elf in the movie "Onward" who has a younger brother named Ian?

998. Leatherbacks, Ridley, and Hawksbill are all types of what reptile?

999. What character has appeared in the most Disney movies and short films?

1000. Which state produces the most cheese each year?

Answers

995) Asteroid
997) Barley Lightfoot
999) Donald Duck*

996) Mt. St. Helens
998) Turtles
1000) Wisconsin

*Donald has appeared in 197, while Mickey Mouse has appeared in 167 (as of March, 2022).

ABOUT THE CO-AUTHORS

Lucy C. Griffith: Lucy is a third grader at Riverview Elementary in Durango, Colorado. She enjoys skiing, playing soccer, and reading. Her favorite movie is "Alex and Me," and her favorite band is "Imagine Dragons." Lucy is also a fan of watching the Olympics and "The Undercover Book List."

Joci Barnes: Joci is a sixth grader at Madison Middle School in Eugene, Oregon. She loves music that is upbeat and you can dance to. Her favorite movie is "Encanto," and her favorite Television show is "Chicago Fire," as she plans on being a firefighter when she grows up. She also enjoys soccer, anime, and math!

Mason A. Funes: Mason is a seventh grader at Signature Preparatory Charter in Henderson, Nevada. Mason loves Coding and Gaming. His favorite book is "Tales Dark and Grim" and his favorite Movie is "Ready Player 1." Mason also enjoys listening to the music of Rex Orange County.

Sawyer E. Funes: Sawyer is an eighth grader at Signature Preparatory Charter in Henderson, Nevada who loves drawing, gaming, and biking. He enjoys Magna Books, and the music of Alan Walker and Fat Rat. His favorite television show is "Raising Dion" and his favorite movie is "Encanto."

Johnathan William Evans: Johnathan is a third grader at Mitch Charter school, and lives in Tualatin, Oregon. Johnathan loves basketball, soccer, and playing Nintendo Switch. His favorite movie is "Home Alone" and his favorite television show is "Star Wars Clone Wars." He loves Harry Potter, his favorite is "Harry Potter, Goblet of Fire."

Parker Carman: Parker is a ninth grader at the Classical Academy in Colorado Springs, Colorado. He loves skiing, golf, reading, and video games. His favorite book is "The Power of One" by Bryce Courtenay. He loves Marvel movies and "The Office," as well as the music of Florida Georgia Line.

Jackson Boustead: Jackson is currently a fifth grader at Ninety-One Elementary in Canby, Oregon. He loves fishing, reading, and basketball. He enjoys all of the Harry Potter book series and the television show "Jurassic World Camp Cretaceous." His favorite movie is "Percy Jackson: The Lightning Thief."

Coming in the Summer of 2022:

"Timeless Trivia Volume 7: Music Edition"

If you enjoyed this book:

1. Please leave a positive review on Amazon.

2. Please follow "Timeless Trivia" on Facebook and Instagram.

3. Please share the book on your own social media.

4. Please consider buying one of the previous five books in the "Timeless Trivia" series, all of which are available on Amazon.

Made in the USA
Columbia, SC
18 December 2024

49873726R00085